SULZER TYPE 4 LOCOMOTIVES

GEORGE WOODS

AMBERLEY

First published 2023

Amberley Publishing
The Hill, Stroud
Gloucestershire, GL5 4EP

www.amberley-books.com

Copyright © George Woods, 2023

The right of George Woods to be identified as
the Author of this work has been asserted in
accordance with the Copyrights, Designs and
Patents Act 1988.

ISBN 978 1 3981 0197 5 (print)
ISBN 978 1 3981 0198 2 (ebook)

British Library Cataloguing in Publication Data.
A catalogue record for this book is available from
the British Library.

Origination by Amberley Publishing.
Printed in the UK.

Introduction

In 1955 British Railways announced its Modernisation Plan, which proposed the elimination of steam traction sometime in the mid-1970s by electrification of the busiest routes and the introduction of diesel power on all other services. The plan was to order prototype diesel and electric locos from the main British manufacturer before picking the best ones for large-scale introduction into BR service, but like a lot of good intentions this one fell by the lineside. The ever-increasing competition from road hauliers, combined with the beginnings of the motorway system, made it more difficult for the railways to retain their traffic, especially freight, resulting in the worsening of the railways finances. Along with government pressure to reduce losses, this caused BR to rush unproven diesels into service before they were ready.

One of the most important diesel locomotive types that was urgently required was a loco in the 2000–2500 hp range capable of hauling express passenger and heavy freight trains. Several prototypes were introduced, the most important being three 1-co-co-1 locos powered by English Electric 1600 hp engines designed by Oliver Bullied for the Southern Railway, which entered service in the early 1950s. The first to be mass produced was the 2000 hp English Electric Type 4, which became BR Class 40. These were heavily influenced by the three prototypes. They were also built to a 1-co-co-1 wheel arrangement and weighed 133 tons, which compared badly with later types that were lighter and more powerful. Nevertheless, the first of 200 entered service in 1958, and it was soon realised that they were under powered as well as overweight, giving performances that were no better than the steam locos that they were meant to replace.

In 1959 another 1-co-co-1 loco also weighing 133 tons entered service, this one equipped with the Sulzer 2500 hp 12LDA28-A engine, the extra 500hp giving an improvement in performance over the steam locos they replaced. These ten locos, which would become BR Class 44, entered service on the WCML intending to replace the underpowered Class 40s. The WCML was being electrified at this time, and it was decided to keep the Class 40s as they would gradually be replaced in the next few years as the electrics took over. An improved Class 44 design was then introduced and a total of 183 were built, becoming BR classes 45–46. The Class 44s were named after famous UK hills, and the three classes became known as the Peaks. They were put to work on the main line from St Pancras to Nottingham, Sheffield, and the Midland route to Scotland, plus the CrossCountry North East–South West route. Some were also based at Gateshead for service on the ECML to Kings Cross, but the 44s were relegated to work coal trains between Toton yard in Nottinghamshire and Brent yard in North London.

They eventually settled down to give reliable service after some teething problems, especially with the train heating boilers, which was a problem that affected most BR diesels, but their heavy weight and long wheel base put them at a disadvantage compared to some prototypes that BR were evaluating in the early 1960s.

By 1960, with their losses mounting, BR had decided to try and save costs by eliminating steam by the end of 1967, but later that was postponed until August 1968. The search was on for a less heavy diesel electric of about 2500 hp. This would replace the remaining express passenger and mixed traffic steam locos. Eventually, after evaluating several more prototypes, BR decided to order twenty co-co locos weighing 112 tons, powered by the Sulzer 2750 hp 12LDA28-C engine of Swiss design built under license by Vickers Armstrong at their Barrow in Furness works. The locos were built by Brush Ltd at Loughborough and became BR Class 47, with the first examples entering service in 1962. However, the need to replace steam was becoming more desperate and it was decided to place an order that would eventually total 512 locos; 310 built by Brush at Loughborough, and 202 by BR at Crewe. The last of the order was delivered in 1968, and their introduction was largely responsible for the last steam locos going for scrap.

The initial batch of twenty were built with a Westinghouse brake system, but later locos were fitted with Metcalfe-Oerlikon brakes. Another difference to the rest of the 47s was the installation of not only a train heating boiler for steam heating, but also a separate generator to feed the ETH system – leading to the first twenty being nicknamed generators.

After a while it became apparent that serious problems with the 2750 hp engines were being caused by stress failures and fatigue cracks in the crank cases, resulting in expensive rebuilds of the affected engines. This was only finally resolved by the engines being derated to 2580 hp by reducing the maximum rpm to 750. After the engine derating, the Class 47s had, by 1969, settled down to give reliable service, and they could be found working all types of traffic on most parts of the BR system from Penzance to Inverness.

The Class 47 was divided into three sub classes: 47/0 had steam train heating; 47/3 had no train heating provision, being used only on freight services; and 47/4 were equipped with electric train heating (ETH), which became standard on the class. In 1979, sixteen were converted to work push and pull services in Scotland, becoming 47/7, and in 1989 the 47/4 extended range variant was introduced. These were fitted with extra fuel tanks and allocated to work the CrossCountry services alongside HSTs. This variant eventually totalled fifty-four locos and were renumbered in the 47/8 series.

Except for four locos withdrawn after serious accident damage, all the Class 47s remained in frontline service until the mid-1980s, when an excess of locos caused BR to withdraw the first twenty, the generators, as they were deemed to be non-standard.

After the privatisation of BR in 1994, the CrossCountry Class 47s became part of the franchise that was taken over by Virgin Trains in 1997. By then the 47s were becoming worn out, and from 2000 Class 220 and 221 DMUs were introduced that, along with the HSTs, eventually took over all CrossCountry services.

Between 1998 and 2004 Brush rebuilt thirty-three Class 47s at Loughborough, converting them to Class 57s by using second-hand EMD 645 2500 hp engines. Some of these were used by Virgin Trains to rescue failed trains and were known as Thunderbirds. They were named after characters in the famous TV series. Other operators using them are Freightliner, DRS, WCR and GWR. The new private operators that acquired Class 47s were eager to be rid of locos that were nearing forty years old. EWS and Freightliner withdrew the 47s in large numbers as soon as they could obtain new replacements, and by 2000 over half the 47s had been withdrawn, with most of the remainder following over the next twenty years.

The Class 47s can still be found in everyday service in 2022, although their numbers are much reduced. At the time of writing, thirty-four are still used in a variety of duties, and are employed by eight operators.

Many Peaks finished their lives at Gateshead depot, and before withdrawals started in earnest they found employment on TransPennine services between Newcastle and Scarborough to Liverpool, along with various services from the North East to destinations in the West Country. They were gradually replaced by 125s and other modern DMU types, and the last examples were withdrawn in 1984.

In the early days of modernisation, many enthusiasts and the public at large said that diesel locos would not be able to last as long as their steam predecessors, but after solving the initial problems the Class 47s in particular have served Britain's railways well, lasting in some cases for nearly sixty years. Many can be found on heritage lines, and if you are lucky can still be seen in everyday mainline service.

Abbreviations
BR: British Railways (from 1965, British Rail)
DMU: Diesel Multiple Unit
DRS: Direct Railway Services
ECML: East Coast Main Line
EMD: Electro-Motive Division (USA)
ETH: Electric Train Heating
EWS: English-Welsh-Scottish Railways
GWR: Great Western Railway
NYMR: North Yorkshire Moors Railway
WCML: West Coast Main Line
WCRC: West Coast Railways Company

Classes 44, 45 and 46

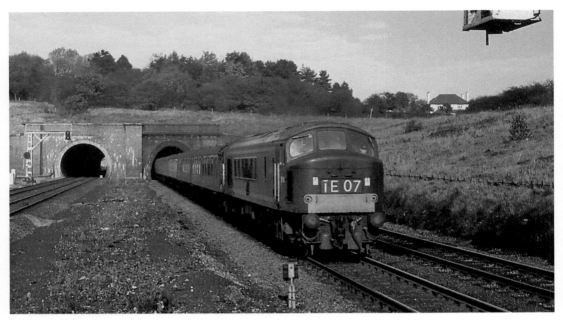

A Peak class loco is into the last few miles of its journey with the 09.00 Bradford to London Kings Cross as it passes through Hadley Wood station on 21 October 1966.

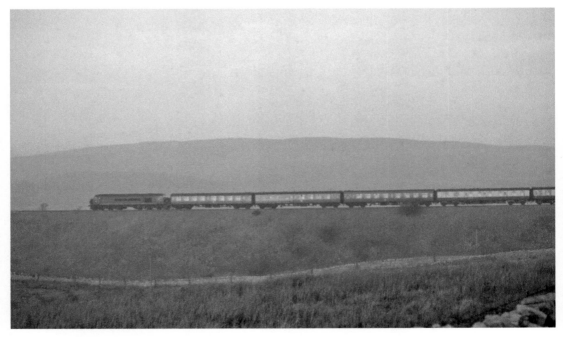

An unidentified Peak heads north at sunset through Ribblehead towards the famous viaduct on 18 November 1967 with the St Pancras to Glasgow Thames Clyde express.

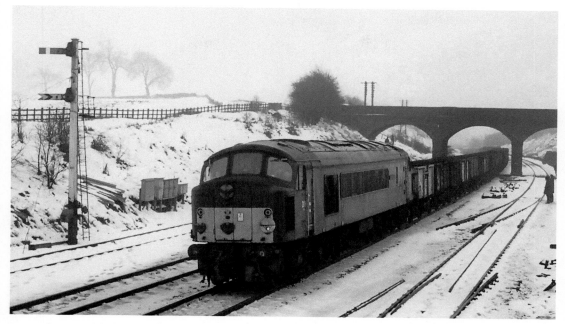

Above and below: Two pictures taken at Kibworth, just south of Leicester, on 22 February 1969. First is D1 *SCAFELL PIKE*, passing the signal box with coal empties returning to the Nottinghamshire collieries. Second is an unidentified Peak passing in the gathering murk with a St Pancras to Derby train.

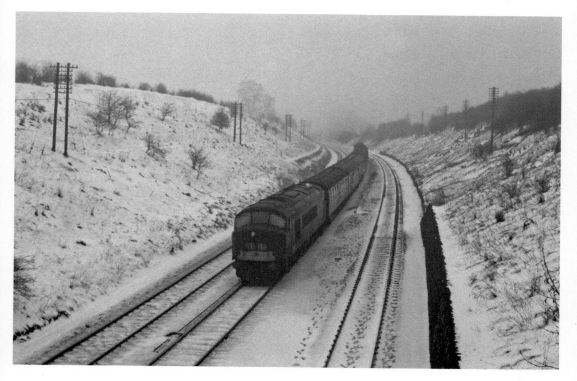

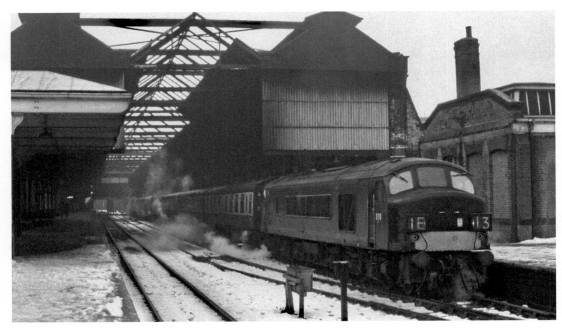

Above and below: Two pictures taken at Leicester London Road on 22 February 1969, showing the station and its environs still equipped with semaphore signals that lasted into the 1980s. First D70 waits to depart with a northbound express, and shortly after another Peak arrives with a train for St Pancras.

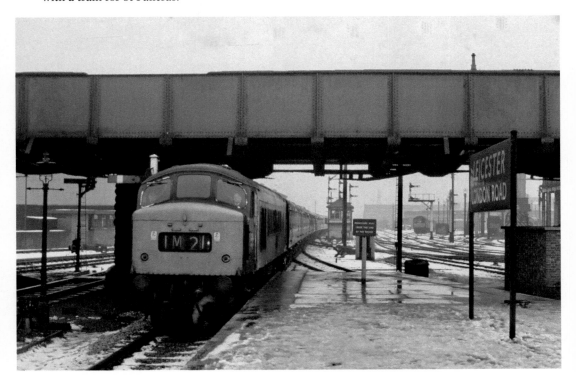

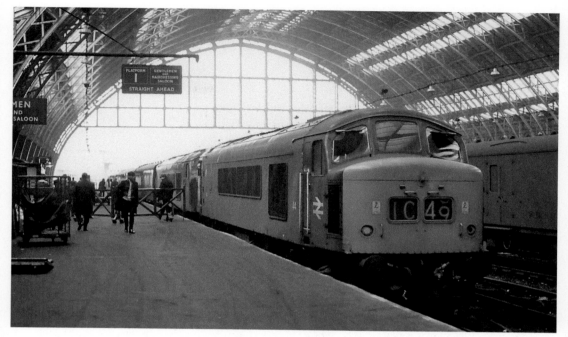

44 double-headed with another Peak, have just arrived at St Pancras with a train from Sheffield on 22 February 1969.

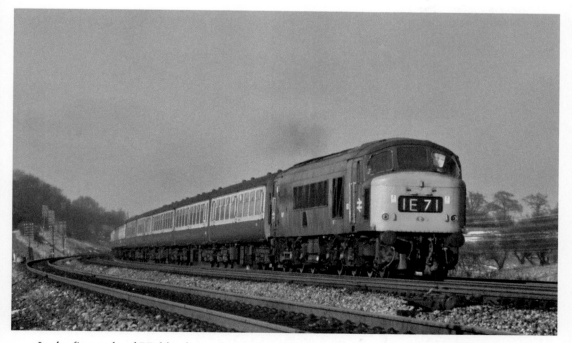

In the first style of BR blue livery, but with a full yellow nose plus a 55A Holbeck shed plate on its nose. 160 approaches Potters Bar with a 11.00 Bradford to Kings Cross service on 17 February 1969.

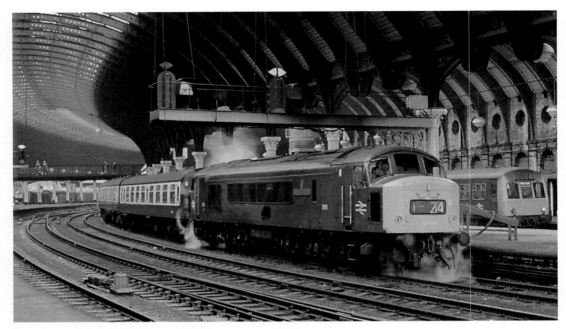

D61 *ROYAL ARMY ORDNANCE CORPS* waits in platform 9 at York station with a northbound CrossCountry service in April 1972. In the background is one of the few Metro-Cammell DMUs fitted with a high mounted head code box waiting to depart to Leeds via Harrogate.

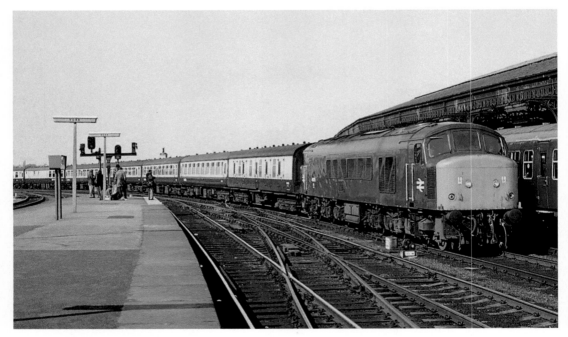

46031 rounds the sharp curve as it arrives at York station with a southbound express in April 1972.

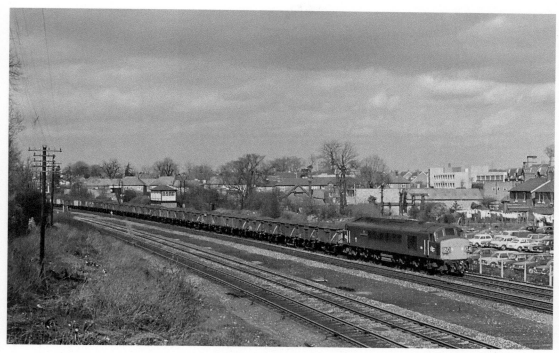

84 *ROYAL CORPS OF TRANSPORT* approaches Elstree station with a coal train from Toton Yard to Brent on 5 April 1973.

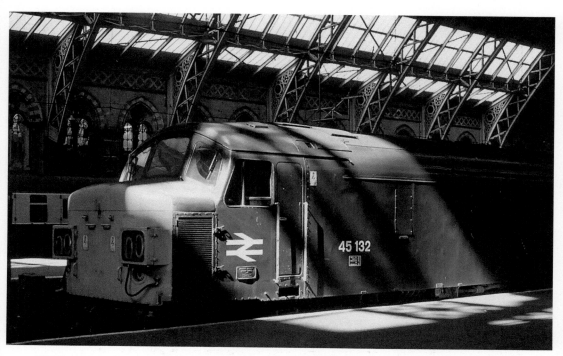

45132 catches the sun at St Pancras after arrival from Sheffield in April 1976.

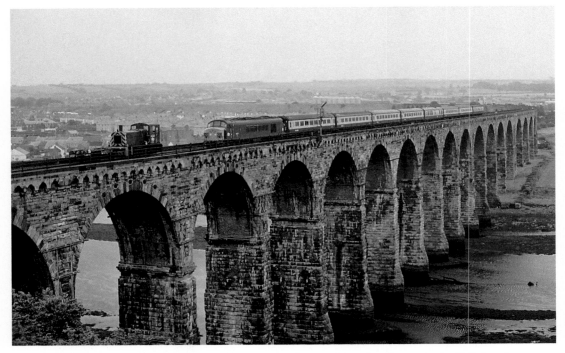

45027 crosses the Royal Border Bridge at Berwick upon Tweed with a train for Edinburgh, as 03066 heads back to its base at Tweedmouth at the southern side of the bridge on 12 July 1976.

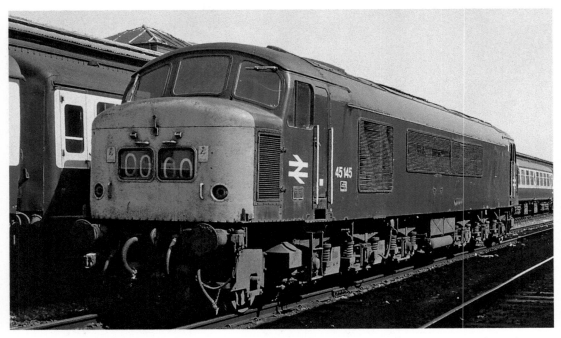

45145 is seen at Reading station in August 1976, and has just handed over an express from the north to a Class 33 that will take it on to Bournemouth.

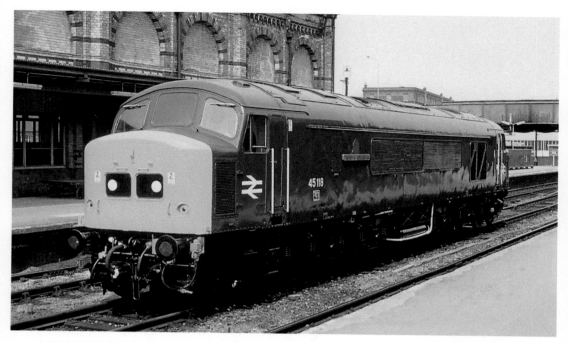

45118 *THE ROYAL ARTILLERYMAN*, fresh from overhaul at Derby Works, stands in the middle road at Leicester station in June 1977.

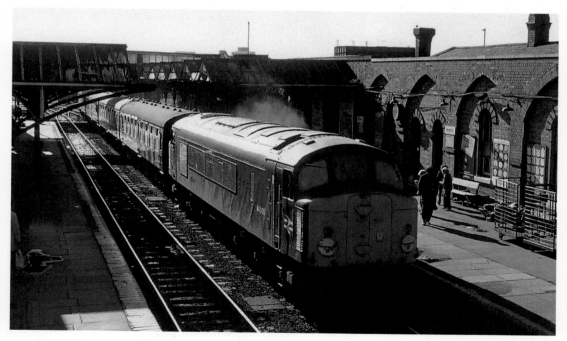

44005 *CROSS FELL* heads the Peaks Express Railtour at Bedford Midland on 1 October 1977. The tour ran from St Pancras to Manchester and return to mark the end of service of the Class 44. 44005 was scrapped at Derby Works in November 1978.

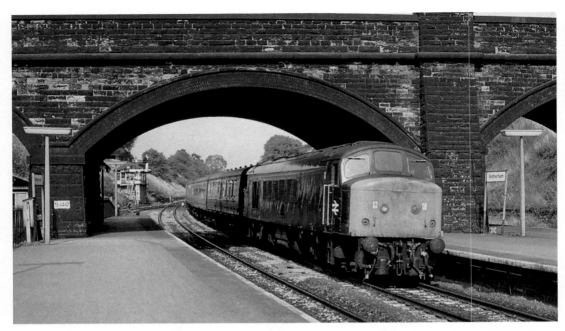

Above and below: Two pictures taken at Rotherham Masborough station on 9 June 1977 of southbound trains passing. First an unidentified Class 46 heads through, followed by 45039 *THE MANCHESTER REGIMENT*. Masborough station closed in 1988, being replaced by the more conveniently sited Central station.

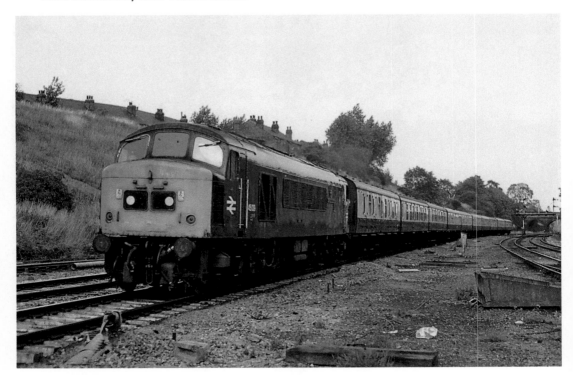

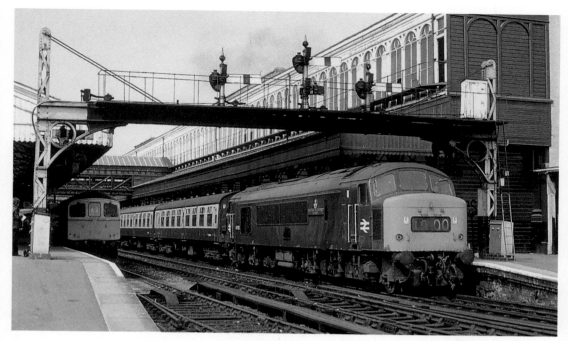

46026 *Leicestershire and Derbyshire Yeomanry* waits at Exeter St Davids station with a train from the north of England to Paignton on 13 July 1977. A Class 33 on the left waits to depart for London Waterloo.

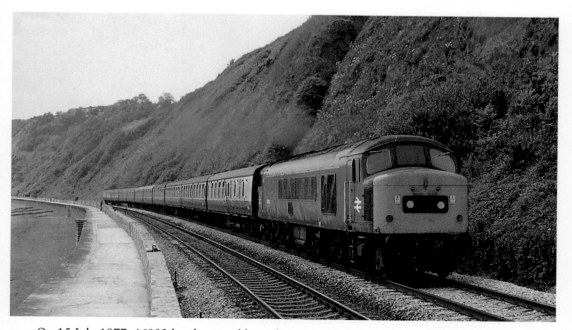

On 15 July 1977, 46002 heads a northbound service along the seawall between Teignmouth and Dawlish. This scene looks lovely on a summer day, but in the winter gales, heavy storms can cause serious damage to this stretch of line.

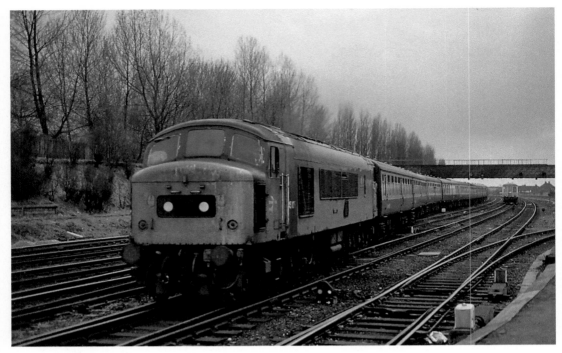

45105 passes Holgate on the approach to York station with a northbound train in May 1979. Waiting to follow is a Class 122 'Bubble Car' on driver route learning duties.

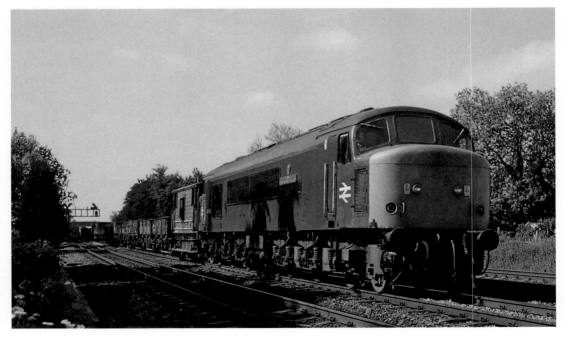

45143 *5th ROYAL INNISKILLING DRAGOON GUARDS* approaches Dringhouses on the outskirts of York, with a spoil train bound for the Civil Engineers yard at Clifton in June 1979.

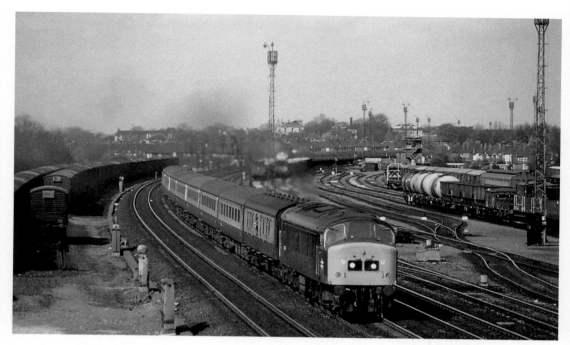

An unidentified Class 45 heads out of York past Dringhouses Yard with a Newcastle to Liverpool service in May 1981. The lines of redundant short wheelbase vans on the left were used on the Rowntrees chocolate trains, recently replaced by modern larger vans.

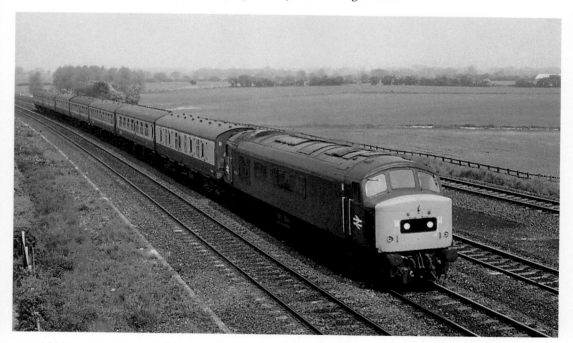

45031 passes the site of Copmanthorpe station, which closed in 1959, with a TransPennine service from Scarborough to Liverpool in June 1979.

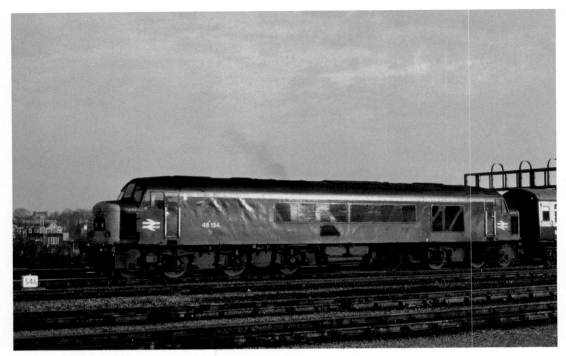

45134 catches the low winter sun as it passes the National Railway Museum shortly after leaving York station with a Liverpool to Newcastle TransPennine train in December 1979.

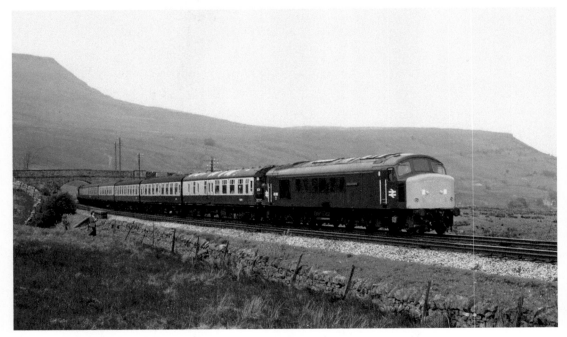

45060 *SHERWOOD FORESTER* approaches the 1169-foot summit of the Settle & Carlisle line at Ais Gill with the daily Glasgow to Nottingham train in May 1980.

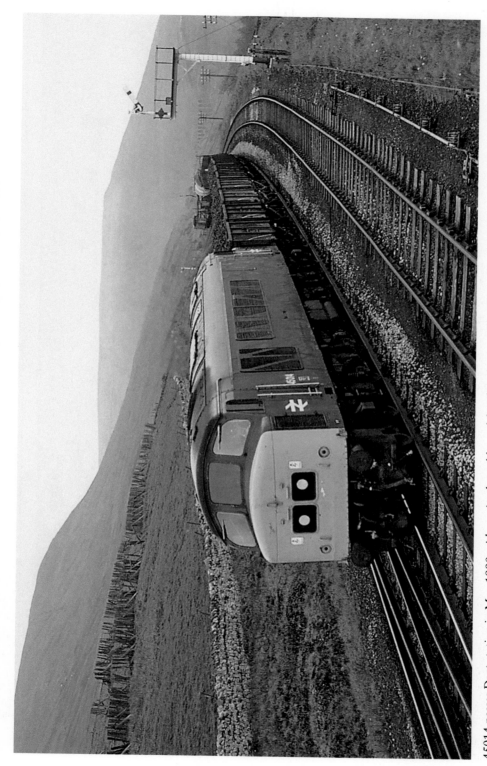

45014 passes Dent station in May 1980 with a mixed northbound freight, photographed from the signal box, which was demolished about a year later. At 1150 feet, Dent is the highest station in England still in daily use. Note the remains of snow fences on the left above the train.

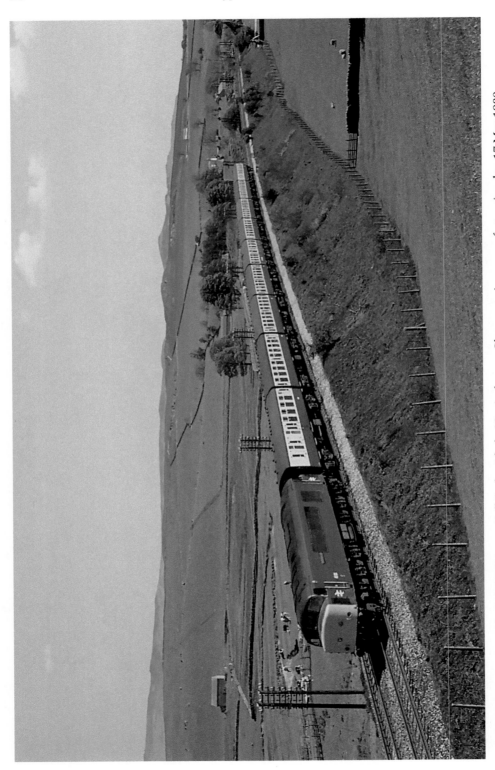

45123 *THE LANCASHIRE FUSILIER* passes Bell Busk with the Nottingham to Glasgow train on a perfect spring day. 17 May 1980.

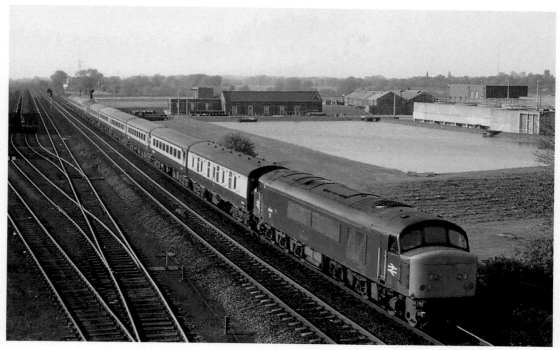

Substituting for a Deltic, 45116 passes the York Water Works at Clifton, with the Edinburgh to Plymouth train in June 1980.

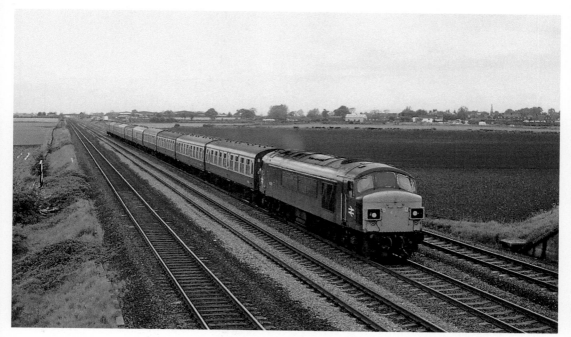

45027 heads south up the ECML through Shipton with a summer Saturday extra train in June 1981.

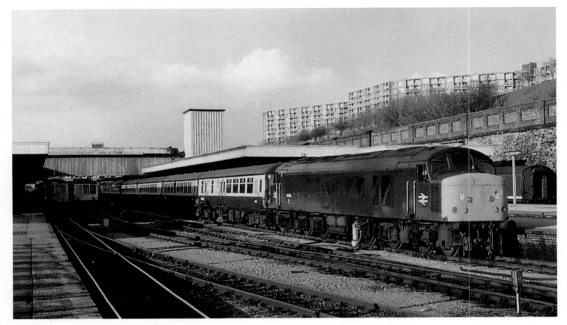

45002 waits to depart from Sheffield Midland station with a train for London St Pancras in April 1982. The Park Hill estate dominates the background and has been part of the scene in many pictures taken here since the 1960s. They were Grade II listed in 1998, and have since seen extensive renovation.

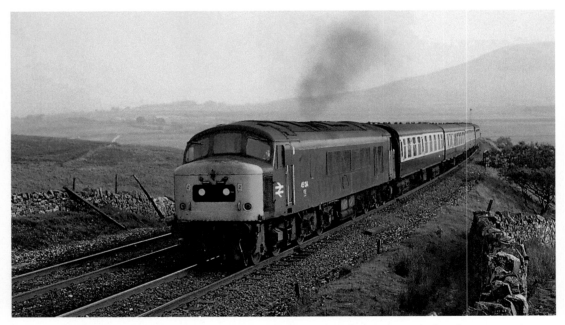

45134 has just crossed Ribblehead Viaduct and heads for Blea Moor, with the afternoon train from Leeds to Carlisle in August 1982. During major repair work carried out between 1981 and 1985, the double track was reduced to one across the viaduct.

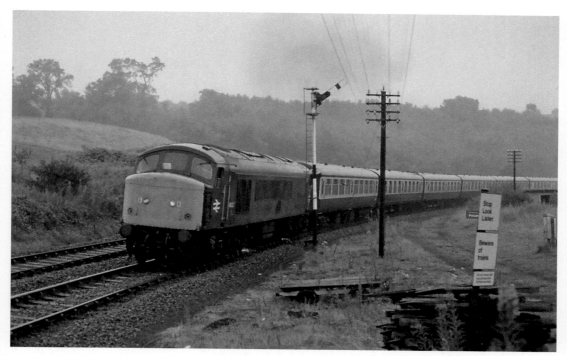

46027 causes sparks as it spins its wheels on the wet rail while restarting a Scarborough to Liverpool train away from a signal check at Kirkham Abbey on 31 July 1983.

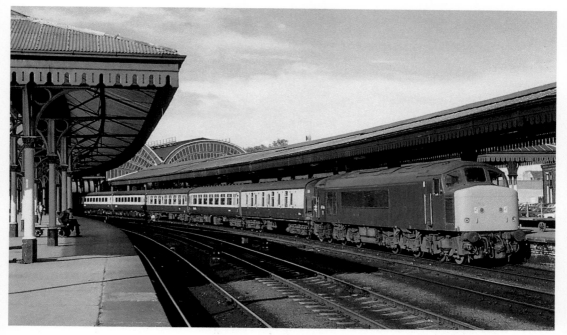

45124 waits to start a TransPennine train for Liverpool away from York station in September 1983.

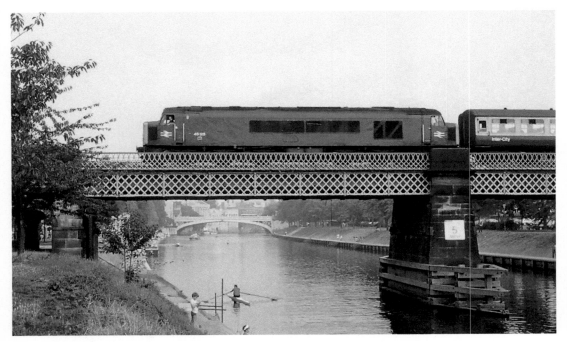

The young fisherman are too busy to take any notice as 45125 crosses the River Ouse bridge at York with a train for Scarborough in August 1984. In the background a York City bus crosses Lendal bridge.

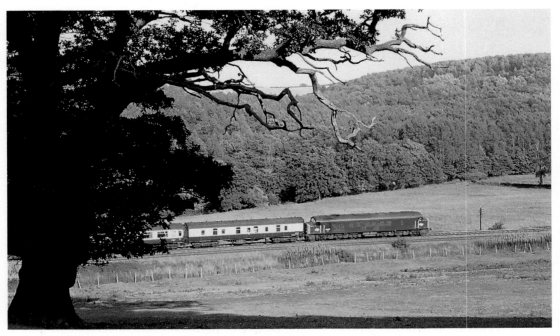

45105 has just passed Kirkham Abbey and heads through the glorious North Yorkshire countryside with a train from Scarborough to Liverpool in August 1984.

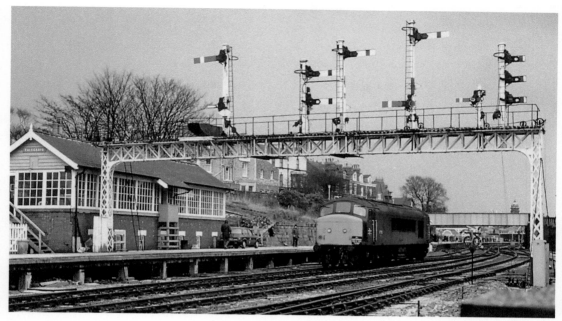

45012 passes under the famous signal gantry as it backs on to the Knottingley Man O War Railtour at Scarborough on 9 February 1985. The gantry survived in use until October 2010, and is now earning its keep on the NYMR at Grosmont.

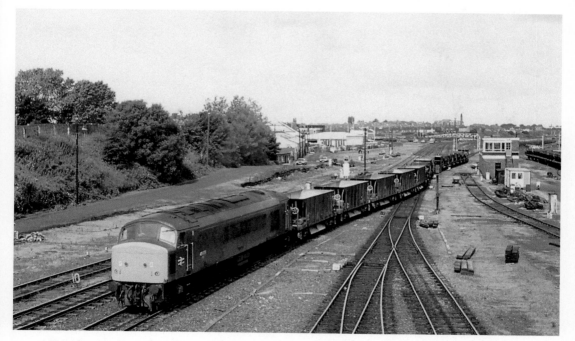

45006 leaves the Civil Engineers yard at York, and joins the freight-only lines that avoid the station, with a train of empty ballast wagons in July 1986. Above the first few wagons, the York Carriage Works that closed in 2002 can be seen.

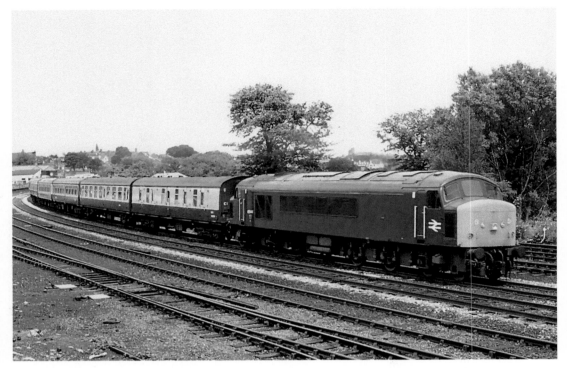

45144 departs from Scarborough with a TransPennine service to Liverpool on 9 July 1986.

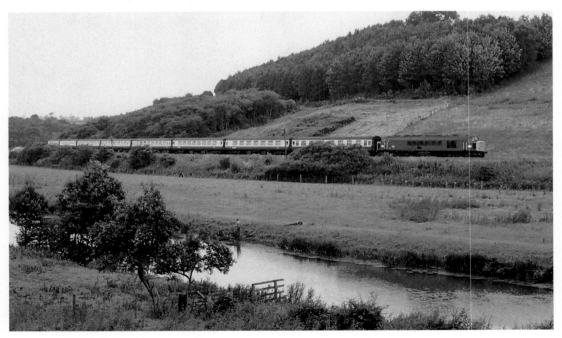

45114 runs alongside the River Derwent near Huttons Ambo with a Liverpool to Scarborough service on 10 August 1986.

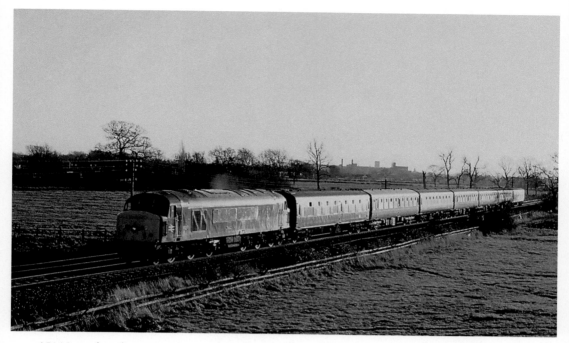

45113 catches the setting sun as it passes Haxby with a TransPennine service to Scarborough on 20 December 1986. In the background can be seen the Rowntrees Works, and beyond that is York Minster.

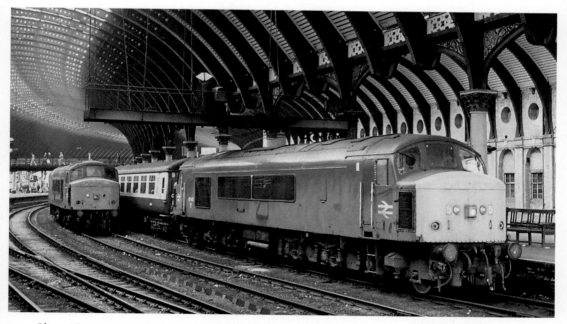

Class 45s were getting scarce by this time, but 45121 on the left is about to take over from 45140 in York station before working forward to Scarborough with a TransPennine service from Liverpool in May 1987.

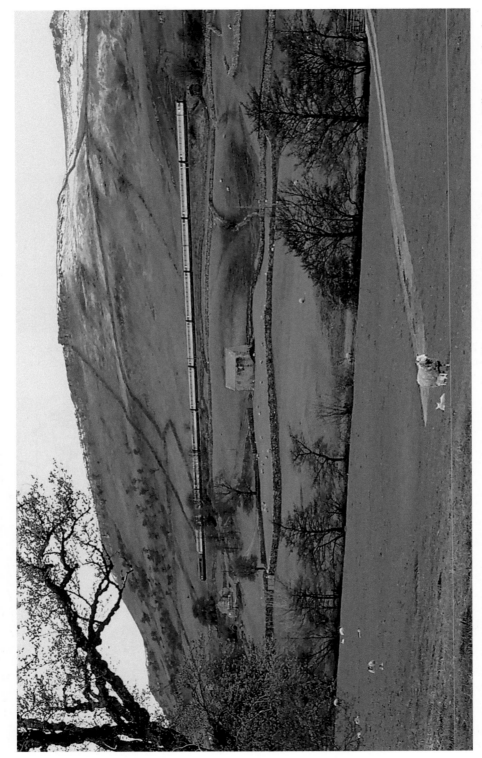

Spring lambs are staying close to their mother as 45124 clings to the side of the Mallerstang Valley as it climbs towards Ais Gill Summit, heading south with a diverted WCML service in May 1987.

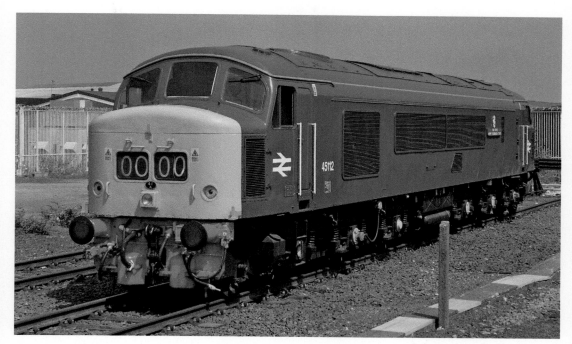

45112 *ROYAL ARMY ORDINANCE CORPS* stands in the siding on the west side of York station on 12 July 2005. It is owned by Nemesis Rail and is currently in store at its depot at Burton on Trent.

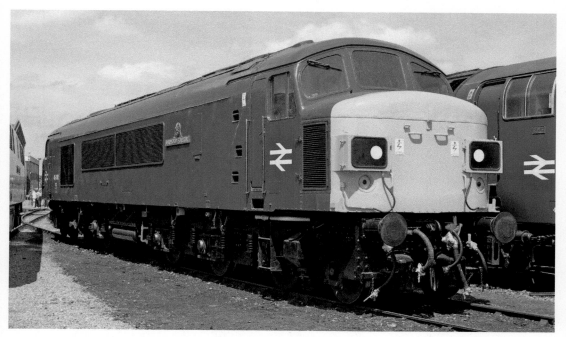

45060 *SHERWOOD FORRESTER* at the Eastleigh Works Open Day on 25 May 2009. Owned by Pioneer Diesel Group, the loco is based at Barrow Hill.

The Class 47s

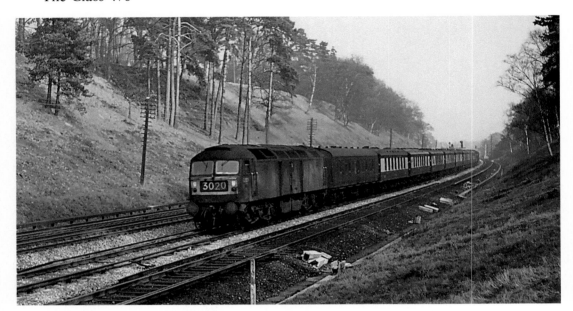

On 14 February 1967 a travelworn D1926 heads through Woking cutting with the Bournemouth Belle. Several Class 47s were transferred from the Western to the Southern in early 1967 to help out the steam locos, which were diminishing in numbers as the end of steam approached.

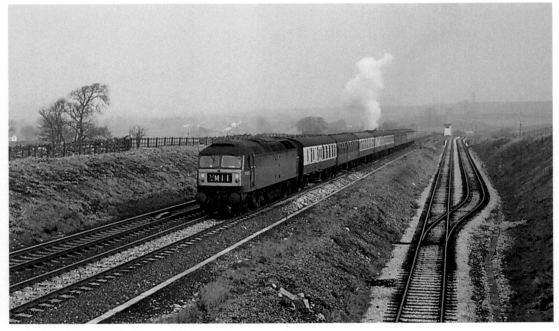

A Brush Type 4 heading a Carlisle to Euston express has just passed Shap Quarry signal box on 1 April 1967. The quarry reception tracks are to the right.

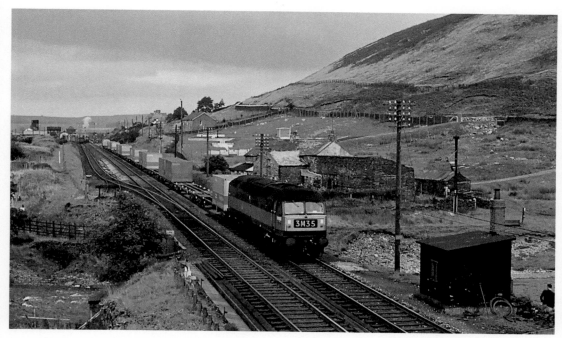

D1653 has just passed through Tebay station and heads for the Lune Valley with a Glasgow to Willesden Freightliner train on 15 May 1967.

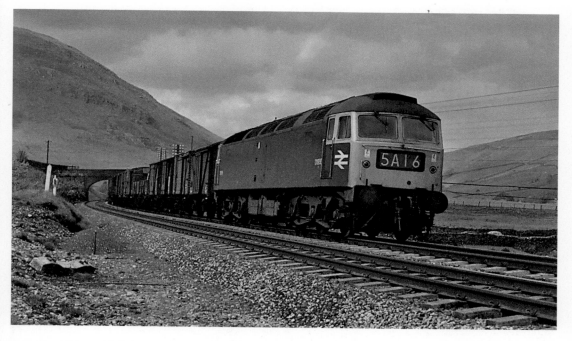

On 15 June 1967 D1956 passes through the Lune Valley in Westmoreland with a southbound freight. Work was just beginning on the M6 motorway, which would pass through the valley along the fell side seen above the bridge.

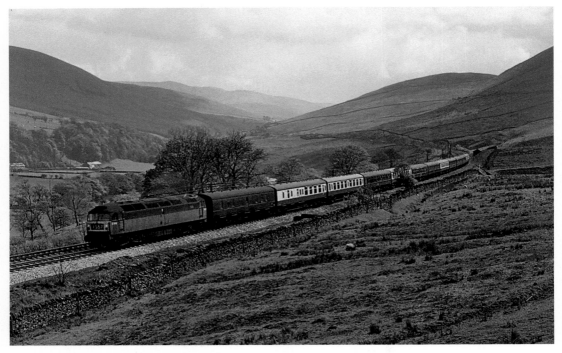

On 18 May 1967 D1846 heads the northbound Royal Scot for Glasgow through the Lune Valley. If I were to take a picture from here today, I would be standing alongside the M6.

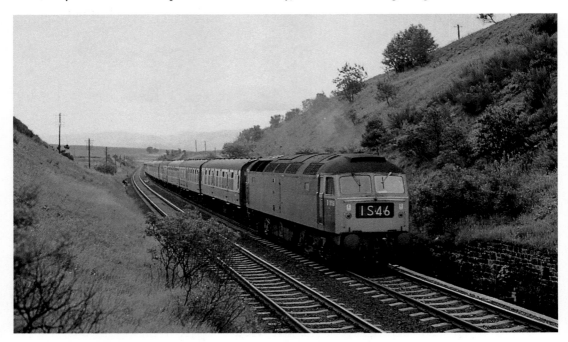

D1858 enters the Summit cutting as it climbs the last few yards to the 916-foot Shap Summit with a Liverpool/Manchester to Glasgow service on 2 September 1967.

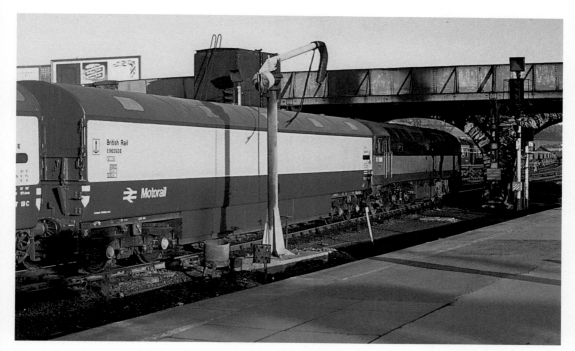

Above and below: Two pictures of D1580 at Perth with the overnight service to the Motorail Terminal at London Caledonian Road taken on 19 May 1967. The first shows the train awaiting departure at the station, and shows the unique double-deck car carriers that were built by Newton Chambers in 1961 and carried six cars. The second shot shows the departing train passing Perth MPD.

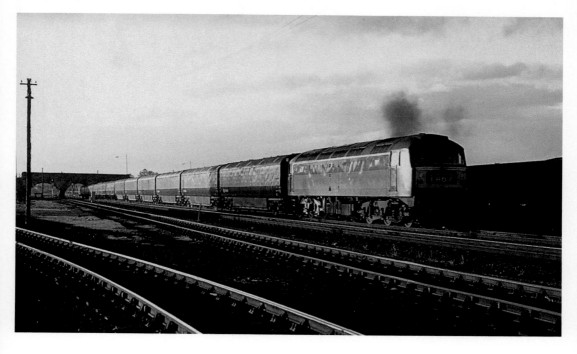

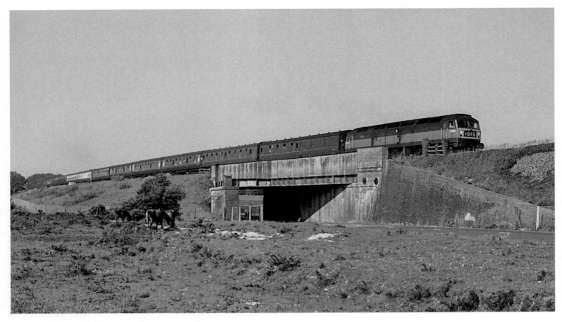

A Western Region Brush Type 4 D1903 crosses the B3055 as it climbs Sway bank shortly after leaving Brockenhurst with the Newcastle to Bournemouth train on 14 June 1967.

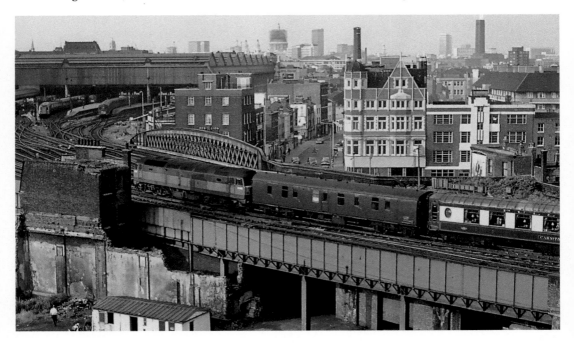

With only five days to go before the end of Southern steam, D1925 arrives at Waterloo on the evening of 4 July 1967 with the Bournemouth Belle. St Paul's Cathedral is among the buildings on the London skyline, and the shell of a building damaged in the Blitz lingers some twenty-five years later.

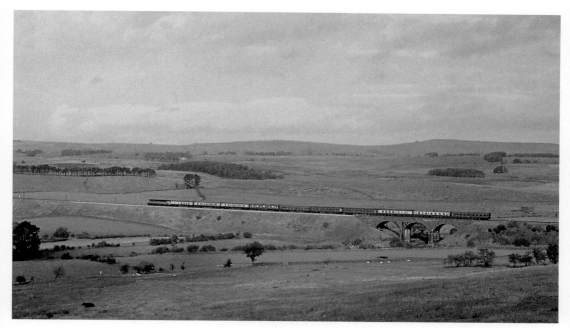

Above and below: Two pictures taken at Greenholme on 7 October 1967. The first is of an unidentified Brush Type 4 climbing towards Shap Summit with a northbound express from Euston to Glasgow, and the second shows D1624 speeding downhill with a southbound train for Euston.

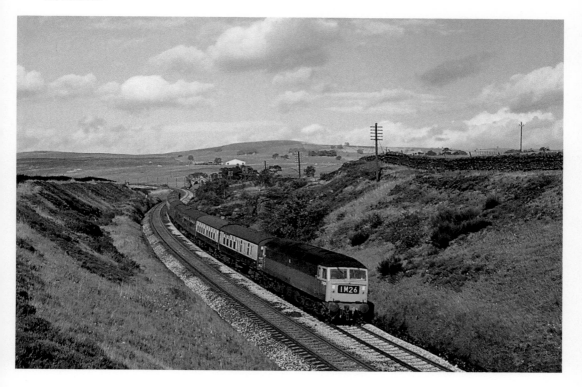

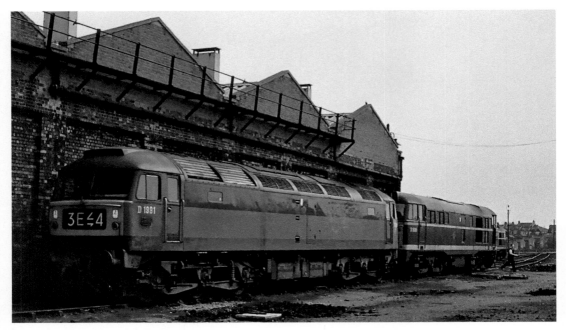

Above and below: Two pictures taken on a Sunday morning, 24 March 1968 at Hornsey MPD. The first shows D1991 and D5595 alongside the main shed building, and the second shows the driver of D1581 checking the front of his loco. Also seen are D1534-D252 and D5595. Today the site is part of the extensive depot that services the EMUs that run on the Kings Cross suburban and Thameslink services.

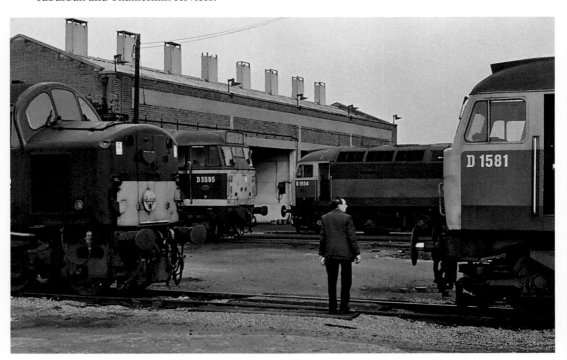

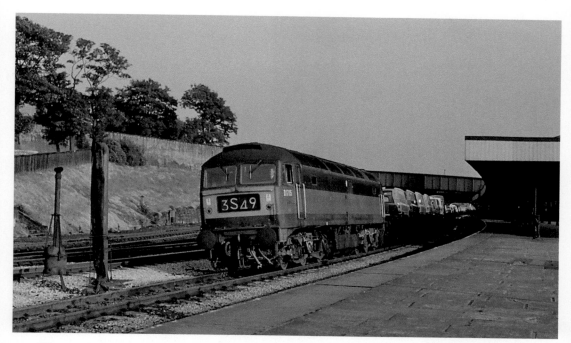

Western Region-based D1715 passes through Lancaster station with a northbound train of motor vehicles on 10 July 1968.

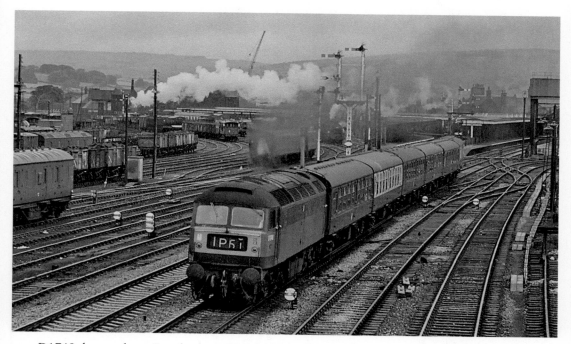

D1748 departs from Carnforth on 11 July 1968 with the Barrow to Euston service that will combine at Preston with coaches from Blackpool. Still plenty of steam activity, though it will finish three weeks later.

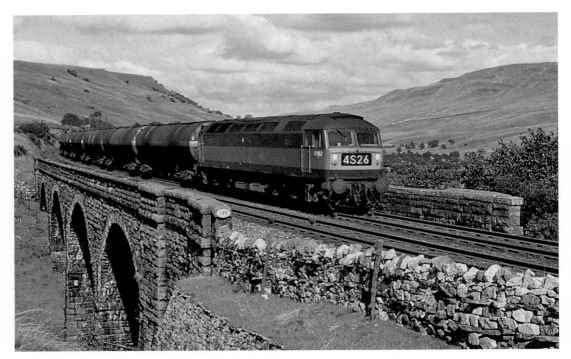

D1952 passes over Ais Gill viaduct and nears the highest summit on British Railways at 1169 feet with a southbound train of 100t TEA tankers on 7 September 1967.

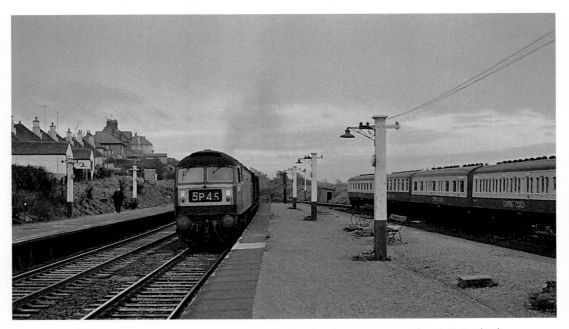

D1740 rolls north through Hest Bank station with a freight train on 11 July 1968. In the former goods yard stand five camping coaches that were hired out to the public for holiday use during the summer months. The station closed in February 1969.

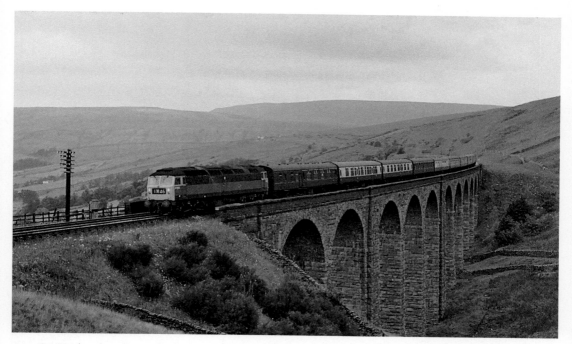

D1824 heads a diverted Glasgow to Euston train over Arten Gill viaduct on the Settle &Carlisle line on 11 August 1968. Following behind was BRs last steam train, the infamous Fifteen Guinea Special. Dent station can be seen in the distance above the first coach.

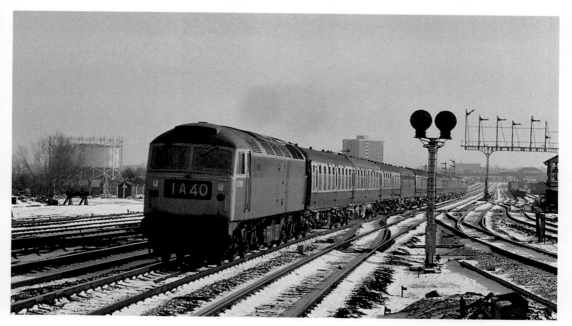

D1764 heads down the long straight from Hornsey and passes Wood Green (now Alexandra Palace station) with the 15.00 Kings Cross to Newcastle train on 8 February 1969. In the background is the Clarendon Road Gasworks gas holder, and plenty of semaphore signals .

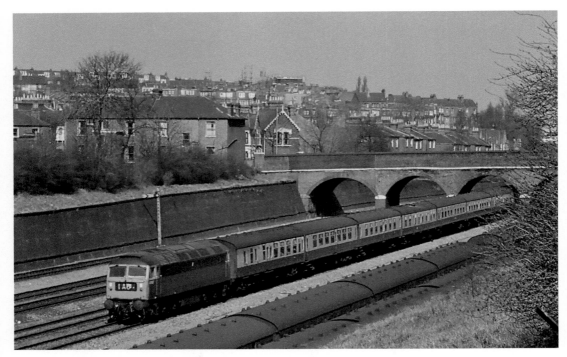

A picture of a Brush Type 4 taken from the spotters platform in Finsbury Park as it covers the last few miles into Kings Cross with an express from the north on 17 February 1969.

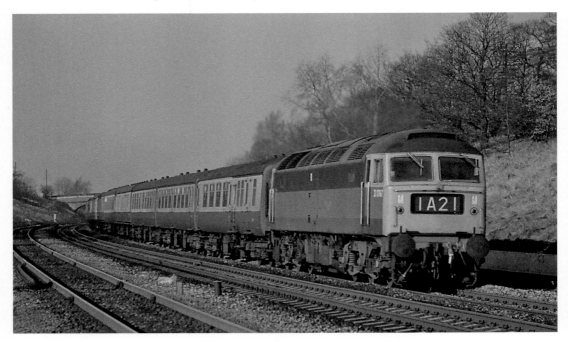

D1767 passes the remains of a recent snowfall near Brookmans Park station, and approaches Potters Bar with a train from Newcastle to Kings Cross on 17 February 1969.

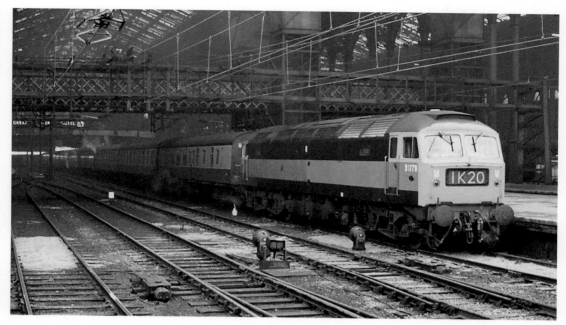

Steam leaks from the carriage heating pipes as D1779 waits to depart from Liverpool Street station with a train for Norwich on 25 February 1969. It's a shame only half the loco made it through the washer.

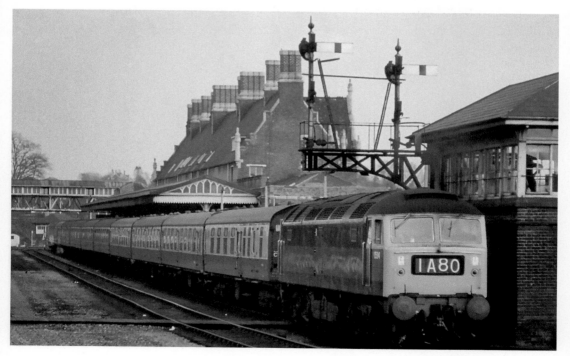

D1594 waits to depart from the Victorian Gothic-styled Hereford station with a train for Paddington on 20 April 1969.

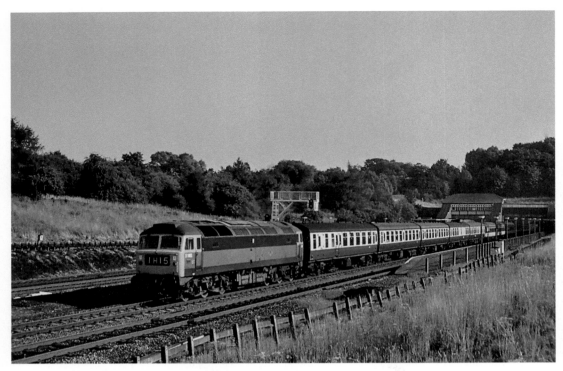

D1103 speeds north as it passes Hadley Wood station with the Hull Pullman on 14 August 1969.

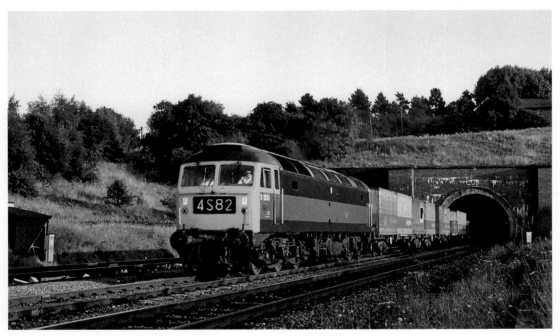

D1985 leaves Hadley Wood north tunnel with a northbound Freightliner service for Aberdeen on 14 August 1969.

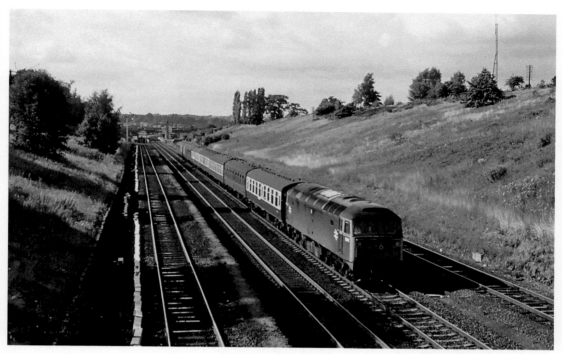

Its downhill all the way now to Kings Cross. 1550 has just passed Oakleigh Park station with a Cambridge Buffet express on 14 August 1969.

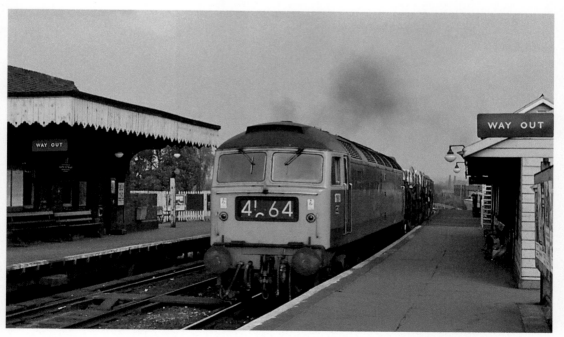

1778 passes through South Tottenham station with a train of Mark 2 Ford Cortina cars fresh from the Ford factory at Dagenham in October 1969.

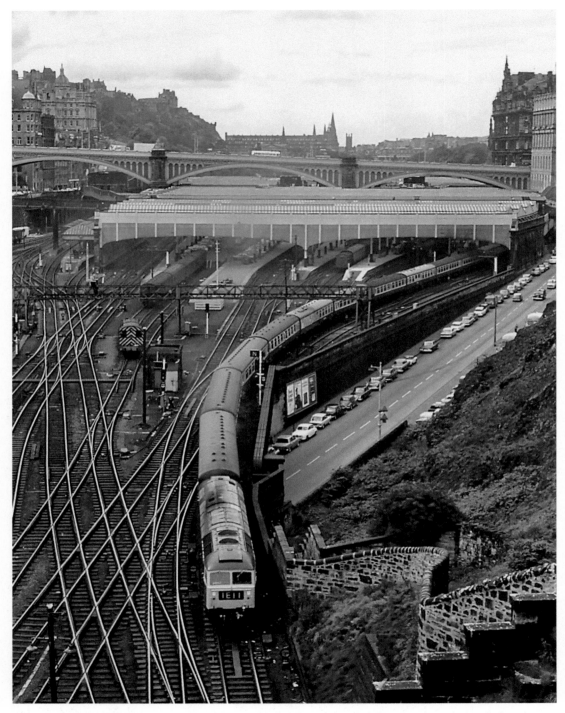

Lying in the hollow between the Old Town to the left and the New Town to the right is Edinburgh Waverley station. The 12.00 to Kings Cross departs behind an unidentified Brush Type 4 on 13 October 1971.

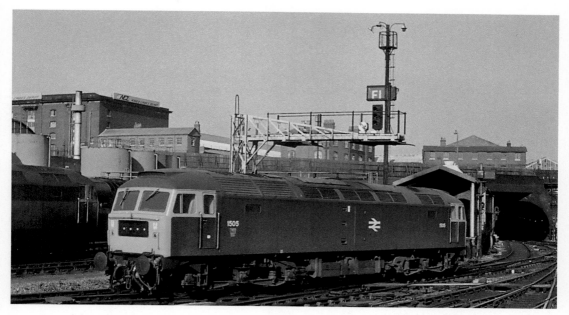

One of the original twenty Generator Brush Type 4 locos, 1505 leaves the loco servicing yard at Kings Cross and heads into Gasworks Tunnel before backing on to a northbound departure in March 1973. The entire area around Kings Cross has seen a huge rebuilding project, which has swept away all the old railway buildings above the bridge, and the redevelopment of the loco yard and the western side of the station.

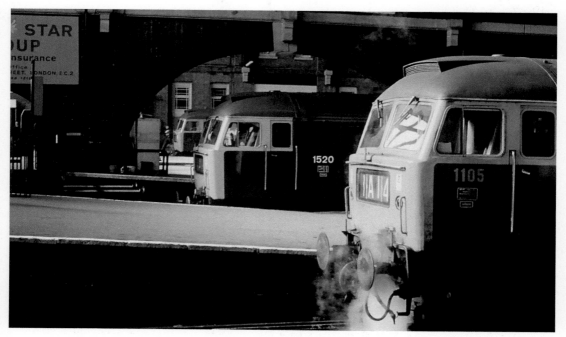

Three Brush Type 4s, including 1520 and 1105, stand in Kings Cross station at approximately 13.00 after arriving with services from the north in March 1973.

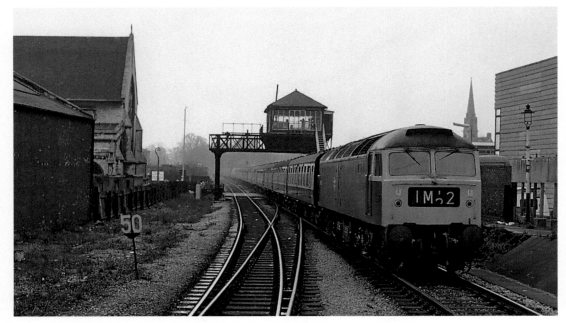

A Class 47 crosses Barton Street level crossing as it arrives at the former Midland Railway Gloucester Eastgate station with a westbound CrossCountry train in April 1974. Eastgate station was closed on 1 December 1975 and services concentrated at the former Great Western Central station.

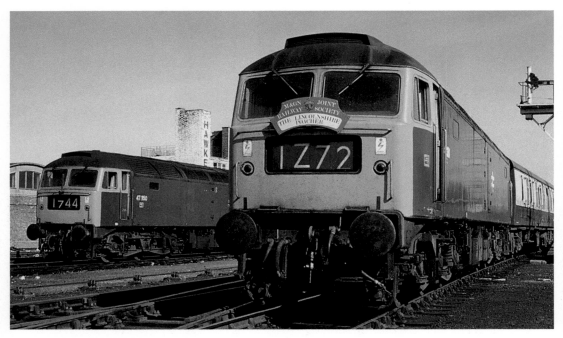

47350 and 47381 are seen at Cleethorpes station on 6 July 76. 47381 is on the Lincolnshire Poacher Railtour that ran from St Pancras.

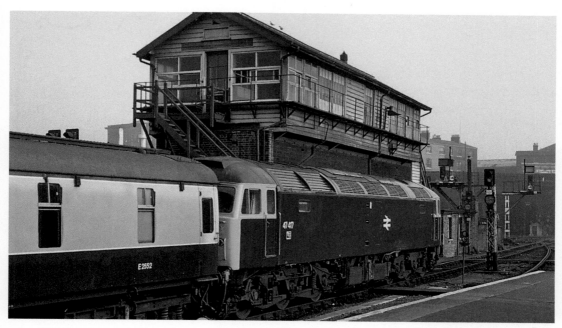

47417 waits in platform four at Kings Cross station to move the empty sleeping cars of an overnight service from Scotland to the carriage sidings at Bounds Green on 28 August 1975. Kings Cross signal box stands behind 47417; this had closed in 1971, but was not demolished until 1976 as part of the big track reorganisation and electrification at the station.

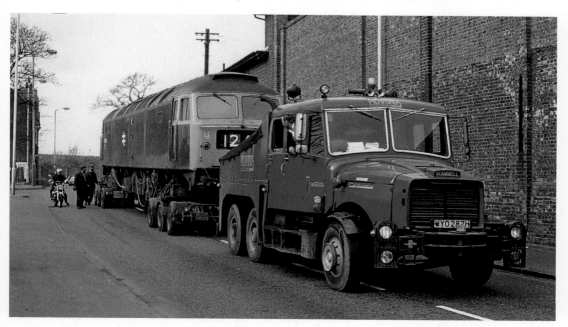

Strange goings on in the back streets of Stratford as 47155, on a Pickfords trailer, is on its way to act as an emergency generator at West Thurrock power station, where it remained for four months. 9 January 1976.

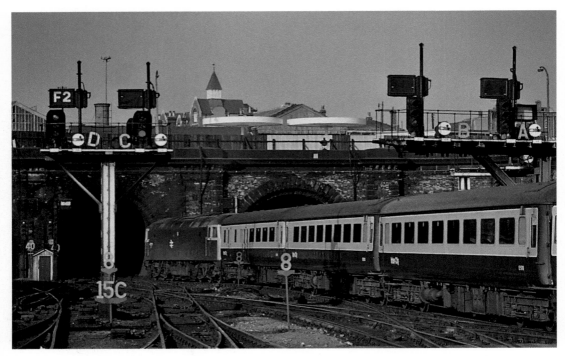

47515 departs from Kings Cross station and enters Gasworks Tunnel with an afternoon northbound InterCity service in April 1976.

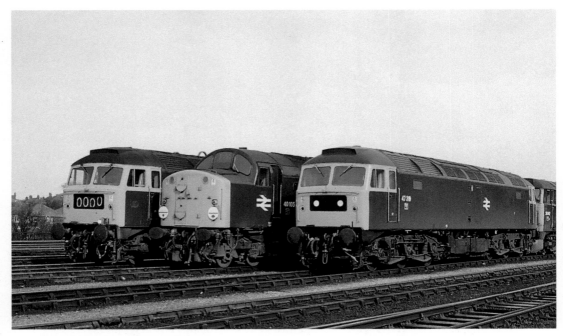

Photographed from the National Railway Museum car park, 40105 is sandwiched between two Class 47s, one of which is 47319, at York MPD on 11 July 1976.

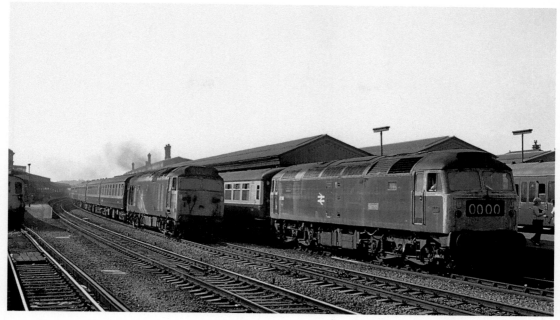

Above and below: Two Western Region 47s, which were named after old Great Western broad gauge steam locos, are seen at Reading station in August 1976. First is 47088 *SAMSON* being overtaken by a Class 50 as it stands in the station with a train for Paddington. Next is 47086 *COLOSSUS* passing through with a freight train heading for Acton yard.

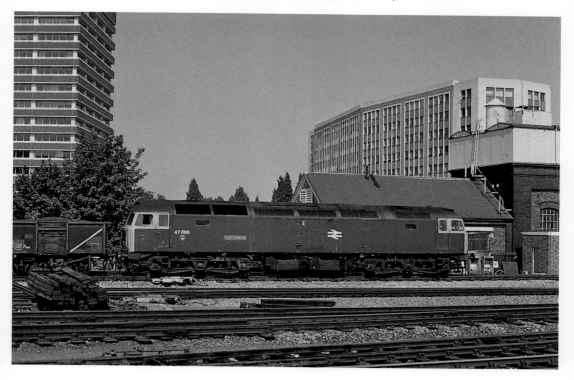

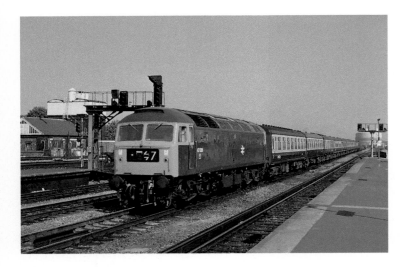

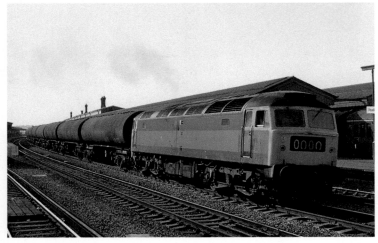

Above left and left: Two more Class 47s at Reading. Fresh from overhaul at Crewe, No. 47028 arrives with a West of England train, and shortly afterwards one of the last Class 47s, still in two-tone green livery, heads an oil tank train probably containing aviation fuel heading to the West Drayton depot that serves Heathrow Airport.

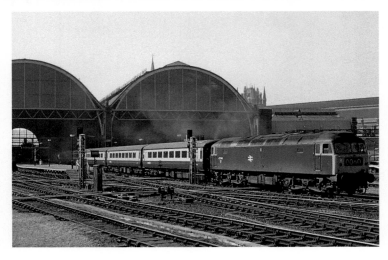

47549 leaves Kings Cross with the midday service to Leeds in September 1976. Work on the Great Northern electrification would soon start, which would bring many changes. More recent alterations have been even more drastic, but have brought huge improvements both to the station and its environs.

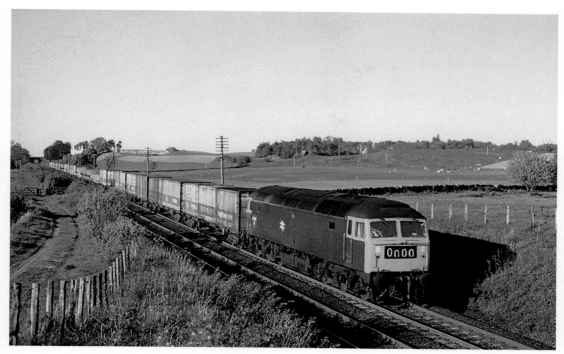

47237 roars south up the old Caledonian Railway main line near Blackford with a lengthy Freightliner train from Aberdeen on 27 May 1977.

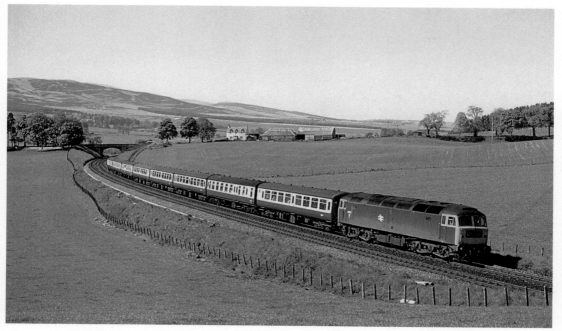

With the Ochill Hills in the background, 47141 approaches Gleneagles with a Glasgow Queen Street to Aberdeen train on 28 May 1977.

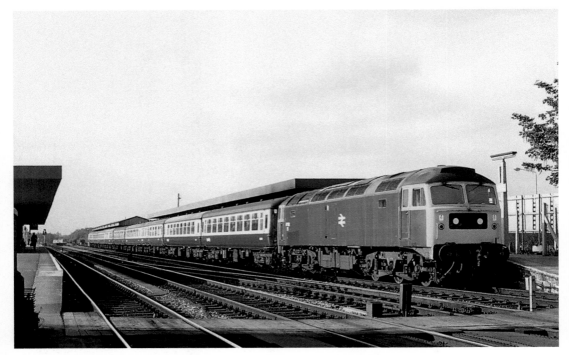

47122 stands at Oxford station with an InterCity service for Paddington on 29 May 1977. Parts of the old Great Western platform canopy can be seen above the rear coaches.

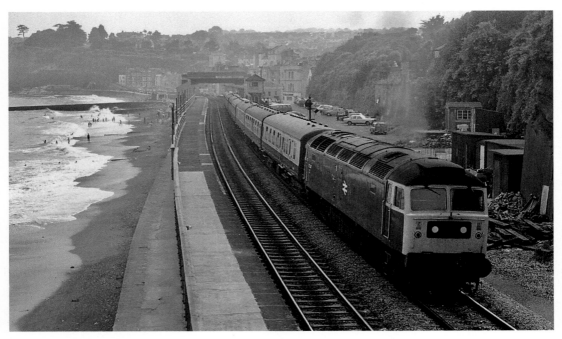

Bathers enjoy the surf as 47247 departs from Dawlish station with a train heading towards Exeter on 15 July 1977.

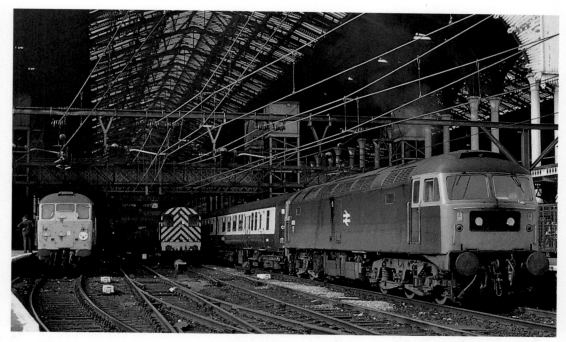

47011 is seen at Liverpool Street station with a Norwich service on 4 July 1977. A Class 30 is on the left in platform ten waiting to take empty stock out to Thornton Fields Carriage sidings, and in the middle is the Class 08, which was the station pilot.

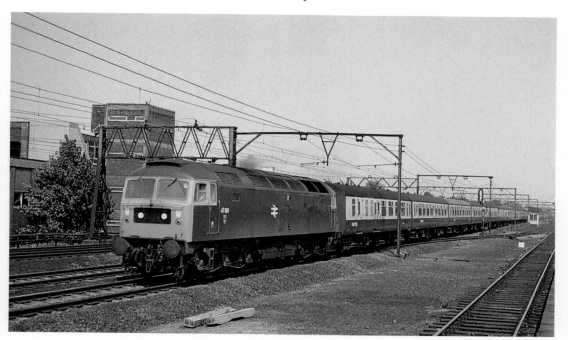

47160 is seen from the Upminster branch platform at Romford station as it passes through heading for Liverpool Street with a train from Norwich on 4 July 1977.

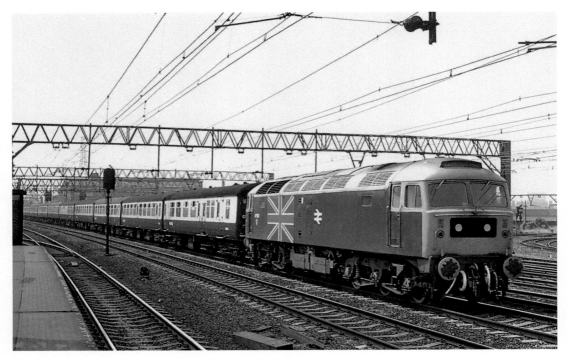

47163 passes Stratford station with a service for Norwich on 4 July 1977. The Union Jack was painted on the loco by the staff at Stratford Depot to celebrate the Queen's silver jubilee.

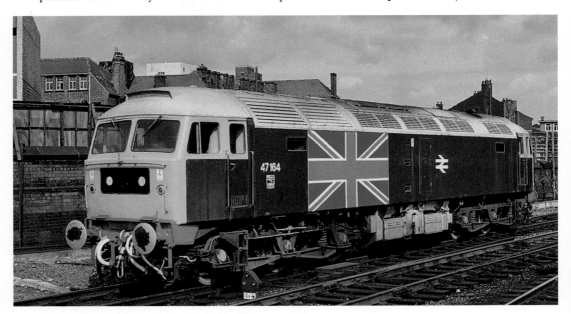

47164 has just arrived at Sheffield station with the continental boat train from Harwich Parkeston Quay and is running round before heading for Manchester Piccadilly via the Hope Valley line in September 1977. This was one of two Stratford locos specially decorated; see 47163 above.

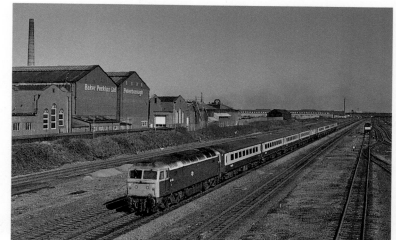

47458 passes the extensive yards at New England and will shortly call at Peterborough with an InterCity service to Kings Cross in May 1979.

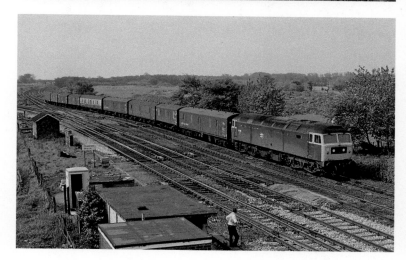

47332 crosses from the Sheffield line to the Leeds line at Chaloners Whin Junction with a parcels train heading into York in June 1980.

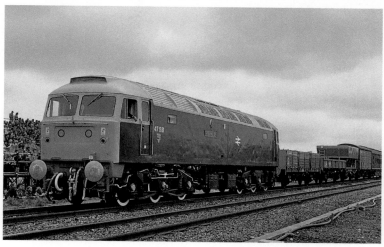

47581 *GREAT EASTERN* heads a rake of contemporary freight wagons, seen here taking part in the Rainhill Cavalcade on 25 August 1980.

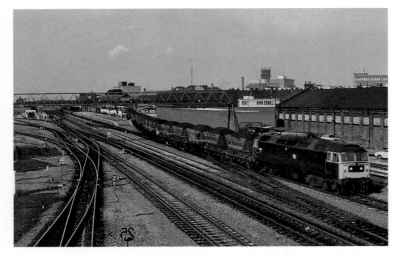

Class 47s were used extensively on merry-go-round coal trains before the Class 56 took over, and 47308 passes Doncaster with a southbound train in October 1981 heading for one of the nearby power stations.

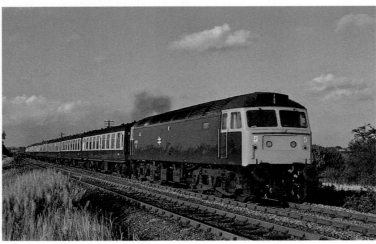

47373 heads into York past Towthorpe with a train from Scarborough in August 1982. The loco is fitted with an experimental orange flashing light above the cab.

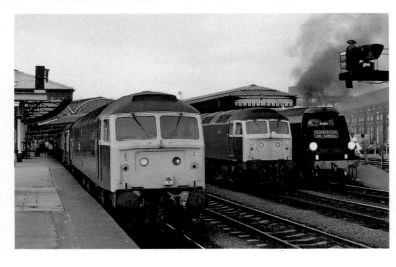

47218 finds itself sandwiched ibetween another Class 47 and 34092 *CITY OF WELLS* at York station in August 1983.

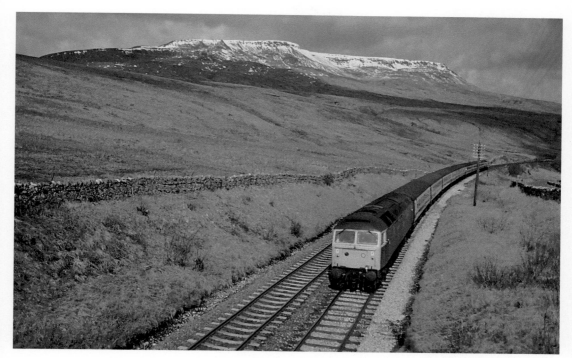

A Class 47 climbs the last few yards to Ais Gill summit, passing a snowcapped Wild Boar Fell with a southbound diverted West Coast express on 2 April 1983.

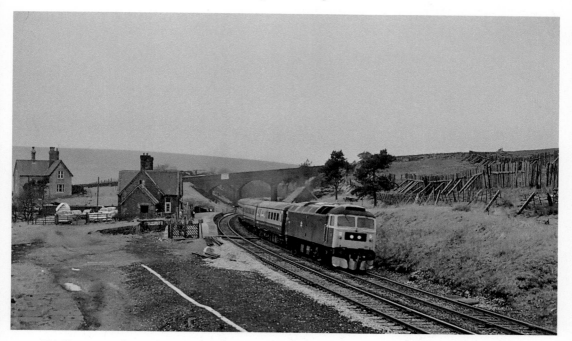

47463 passes through Dent station just before another snow shower starts, heading a southbound diverted WCML service on 2 April 1983.

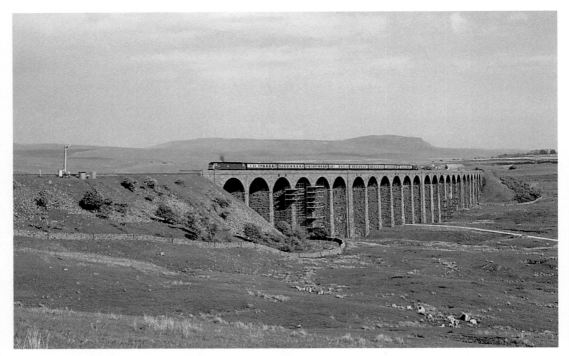

47479 crosses Ribblehead Viaduct in June 1984 with the afternoon train from Leeds to Carlisle. The 2372-foot-high peak of Ingleborough dominates the background

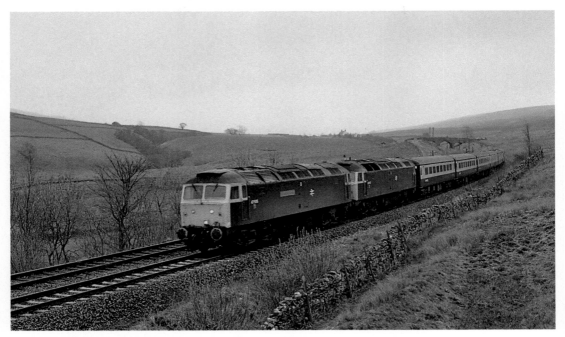

47535 *UNIVERSITY OF LEICESTER* and 47447 start the downhill run to Appleby and Carlisle from Ais Gill summit on 4 May 1985 with a diverted WCML train.

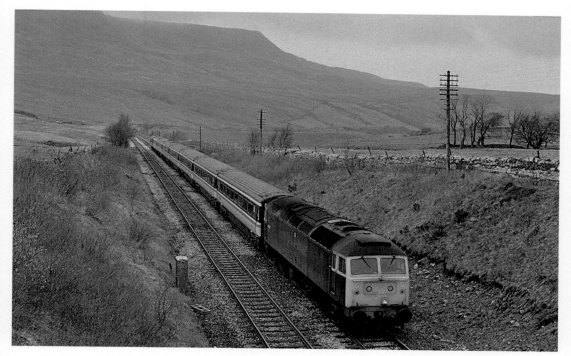

47305 is at the 1169-foot summit of the Settle & Carlisle line at Ais Gill on 4 May 1985 with the diverted Royal Scot Glasgow to Euston train.

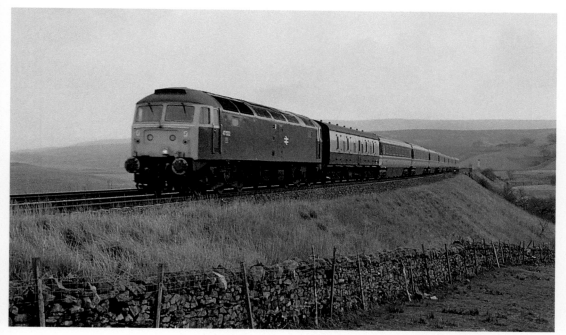

47532 accelerates away from Moorcock tunnel and Lunds viaduct with another diverted Euston to Glasgow train on 4 May 1985.

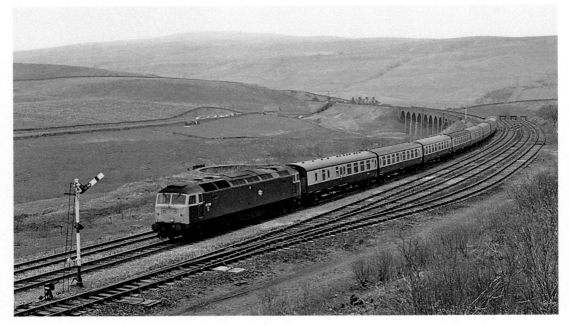

47145 leaves Garsdale viaduct behind and approaches the station with a southbound train on 4 May 1985. The remains of the infamous turntable can be seen above 47145. It is said that in 1900 the Helm wind took hold of a loco on the turntable and blew it around for some time before the crew could regain control.

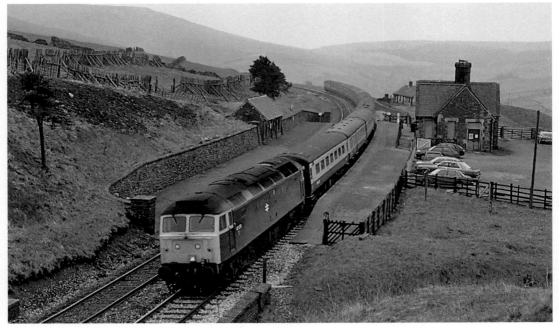

47479 roars north through Dent station on 4 May 1985. The station is 400 feet above the village of Dent, and 5 miles distant along the narrow road that twists along the valley floor.

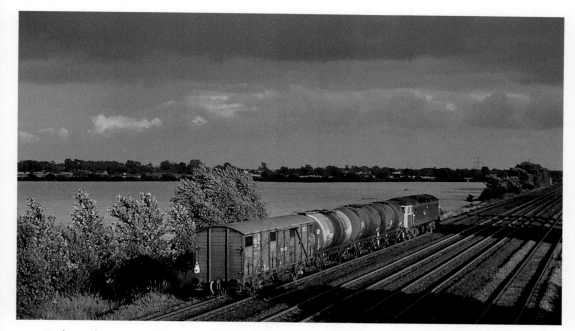

Under a threatening sky, an unidentified Class 47 heads a short freight down the ECML at Shipton in August 1985. The last wagon is a Spanish Transfesa van, which crossed the Channel via the train ferry from Dunkerque to Dover bringing in Spanish onions, and is returning with chemicals from Teeside.

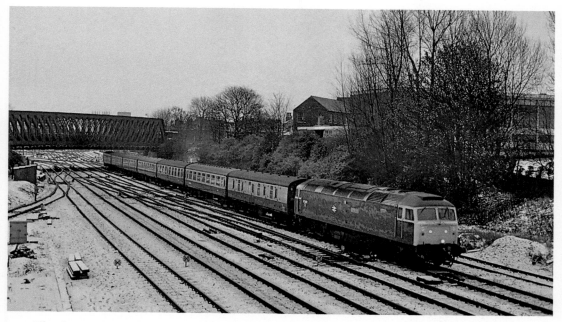

The former D1501, now 47402 *GATESHEAD*, leaves York and passes under Holgate Road bridge with a TransPennine service in January 1986. This loco is preserved at the East Lancs Railway.

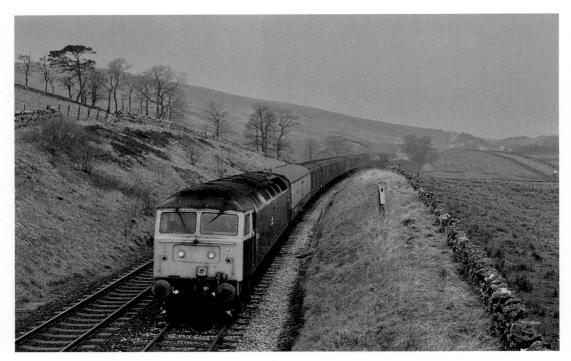

47478 approaches Lunds viaduct with the Stranraer to Manchester empty newspaper vans during another weekend of diversions from the WCML in April 1986.

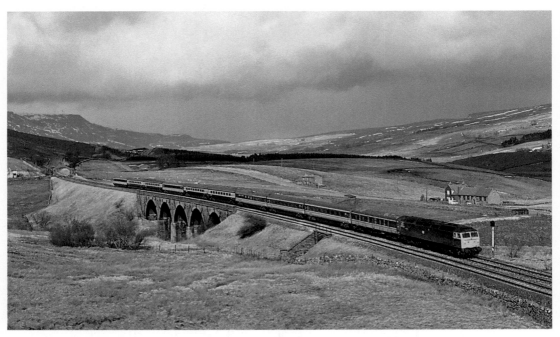

With the remains of a recent snowfall still visible, 47516 crosses Lunds viaduct with a diverted Glasgow to Euston InterCity in April 1986.

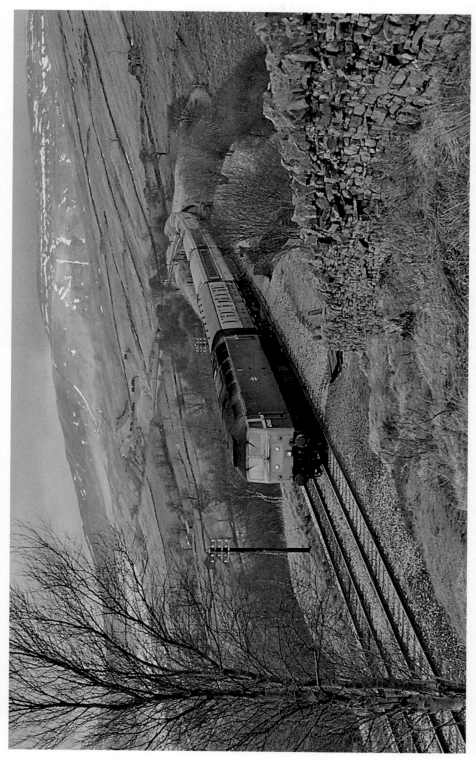

47442 crosses the 100-foot high Dent Head viaduct, and approaches the 2629-yard Blea Moor Tunnel with another diverted Glasgow to Euston train in April 1986.

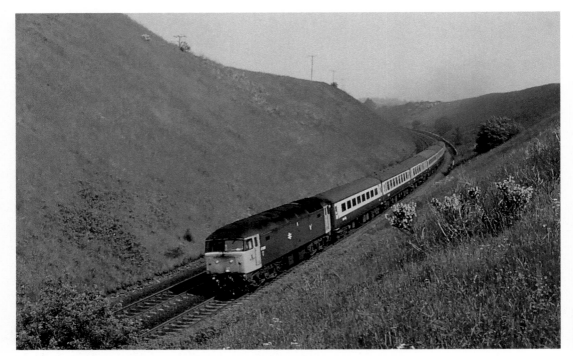

47604 climbs away from Gleneagles station through the Gorse lined cutting with an Aberdeen to Glasgow train in July 1986.

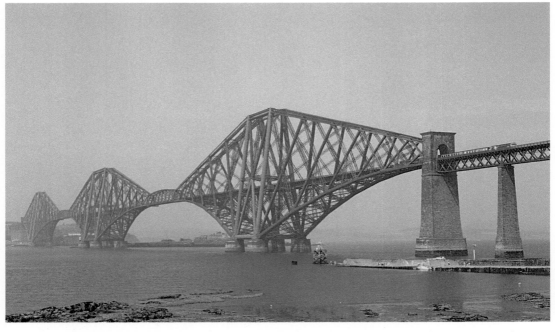

Photographed from South Queensferry, 47450 crosses the 2.5 mile Forth bridge with a Dundee to Edinburgh train in July 1986.

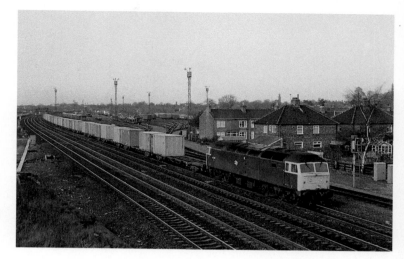

47227 passes the busy Dringhouses Yard at York with a southbound container train in April 1986.

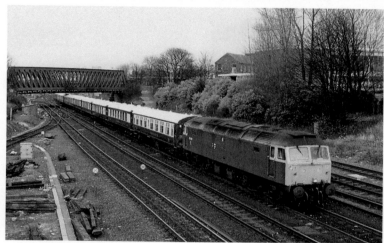

47437 departs from York under the Holgate Road bridge, with the Orient Express returning to Manchester on a luxury lunch excursion in October 1986.

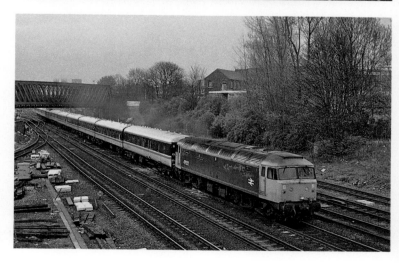

47522 DONCASTER ENTERPRISE departs from York with the return leg of the InterCity VIP Charters Class 40 Farewell Railtour to Kings Cross on 16 April 1988.

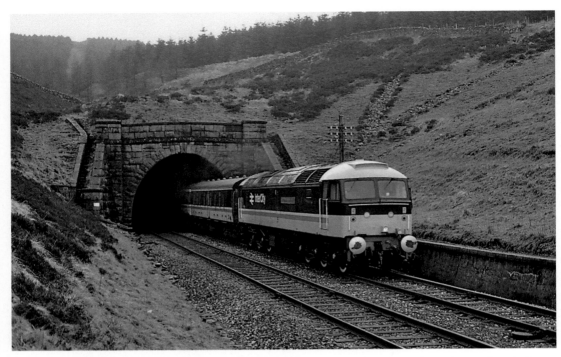

A freshly overhauled 47555 *THE COMMONWEALTH SPIRIT* emerges from the north end of Blea Moor tunnel with a diverted WCML service in April 1988.

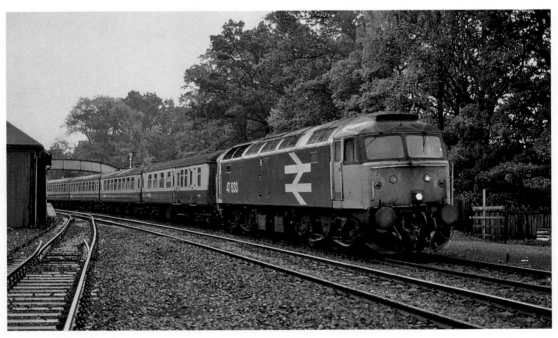

47630 leaves Pitlochry with an Edinburgh and Glasgow to Inverness train on a wet October day in 1988.

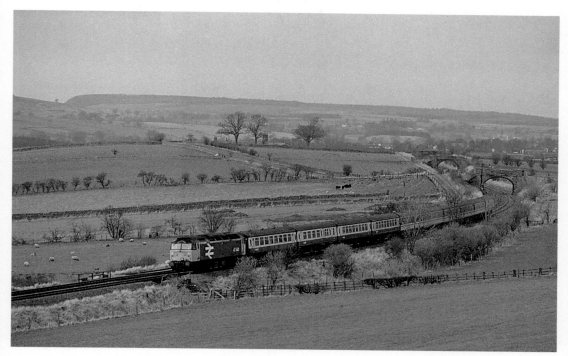

47441 runs up the Eden Valley near Edenhall with a diverted WCML train on 4 March 1989. Note the three overbridges: the nearest carries the B6412, and the other two carrying farm tracks.

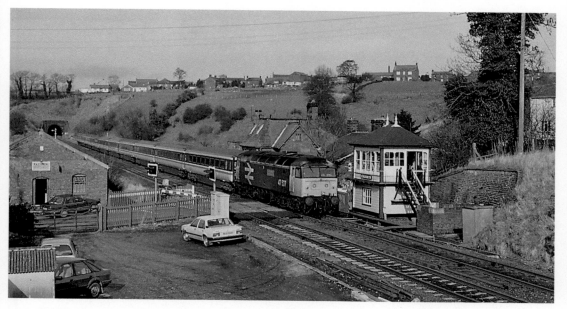

47537 *SIR GWNEDD/COUNTY OF GWYNEDD* has just left Culgaith Tunnel, and is passing the signal box with a diverted Glasgow to Euston train on 4 March 1989. Above the loco the station building, which saw its last passengers in 1970 and is now a private dwelling, can be seen.

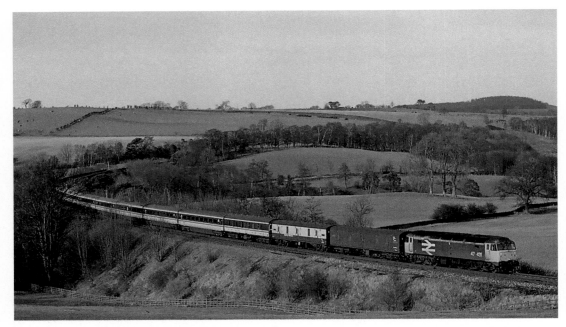

Above and below: Two pictures taken just south of Armathwaite station on 4 March 1989. 47431 heads south with a diverted Glasgow to Euston train that is also carrying cars in the two vans at the front of the train, and 47544 leaves the north end of Armathwaite Tunnel with a northbound diverted train.

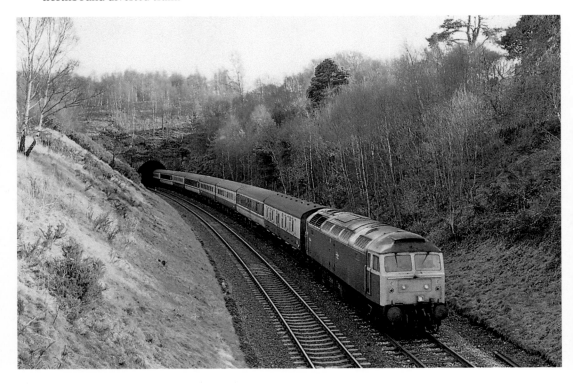

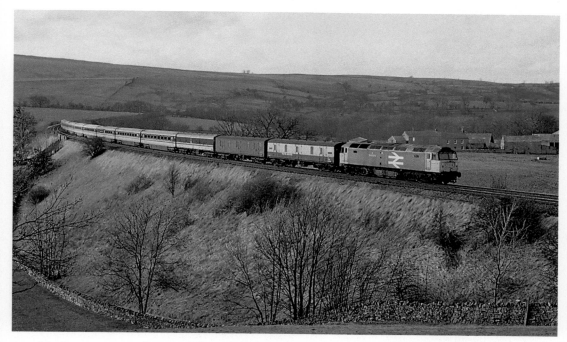

Motive power must have ran short as Railfreight Distribution 47365 *SILVER JUBILEE*, which had no train heating equipment, climbs near Smardale with the 12.37 Glasgow to Euston train, again with the motorail vans on 11 March 1989.

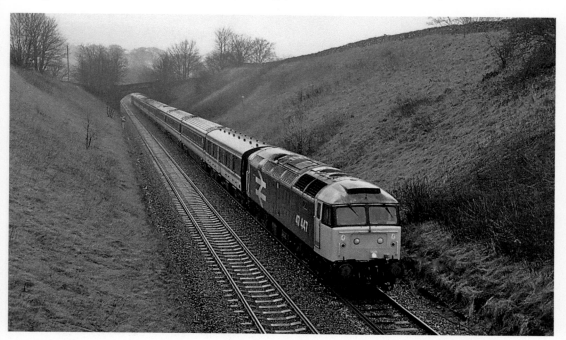

More diversions took place next weekend, and 47447 is seen climbing through Stainforth with a Euston to Glasgow train on a very wet 18 March 1989.

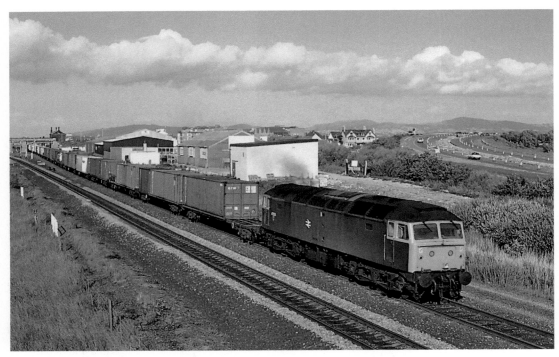

Above and below: Two pictures taken at Abergele on the North Wales Coast Line in July 1989. First is 47333 passing with a container train for Holyhead, and second, coming in the other direction, is 97480 *ROBIN HOOD* with a Llandudno to Manchester train.

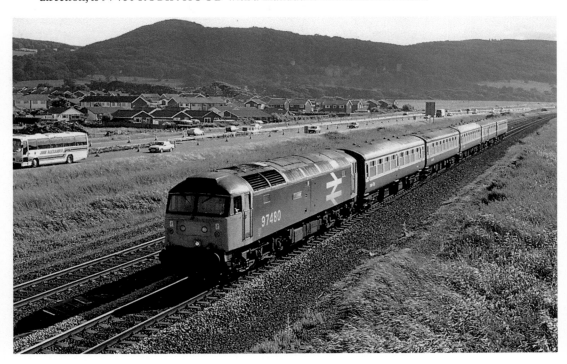

47401 waits in platform nine at York station with a northbound train in July 1989. Originally D1500, this was the first Brush Type 4 that entered service in 1962. It was withdrawn in 1992, and from 1994 has been preserved at the Midland Railway Centre.

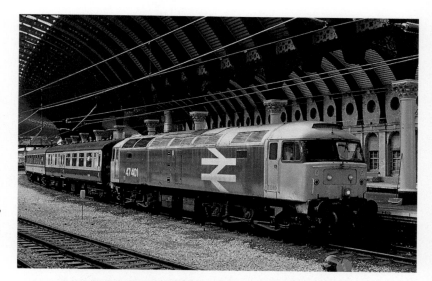

47714, in Network Southeast livery, stands in platform nine at York station in November 1989 with a Pathfinder Railtour.

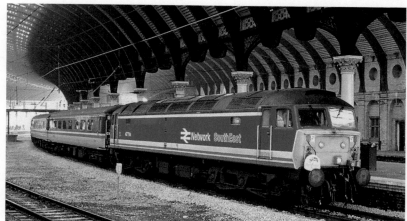

An immaculate 47821 *ROYAL WORCESTER* departs from York station with a Children in Need special that ran from Aberdeen to Kings Cross on 17 November 1989.

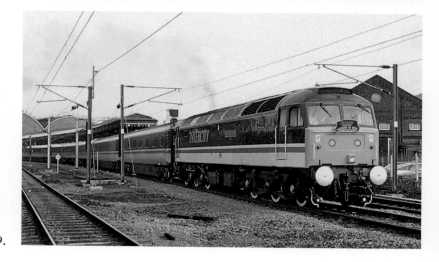

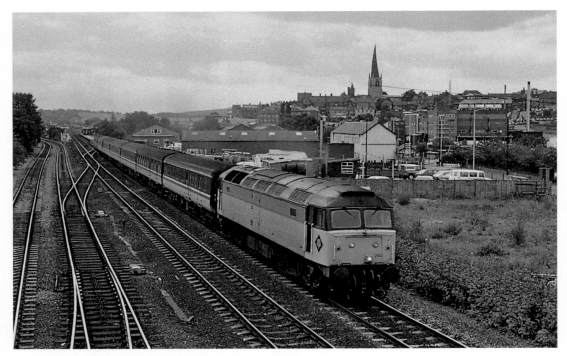

47290 heads a northbound CrossCountry service away from Chesterfield, with its famous twisted spire visible on the skyline, on 29 September 1990.

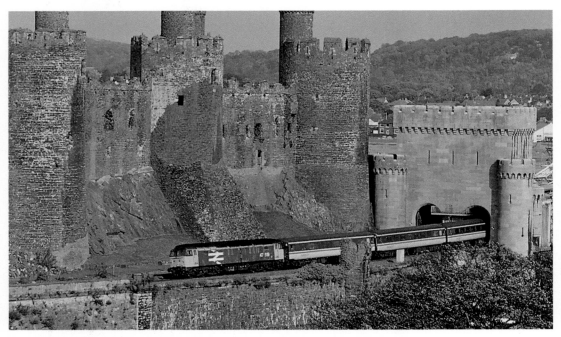

47519 heads a Euston to Holyhead service off of the Conwy Suspension Bridge, and past the imposing Conwy Castle, on 13 October 1990.

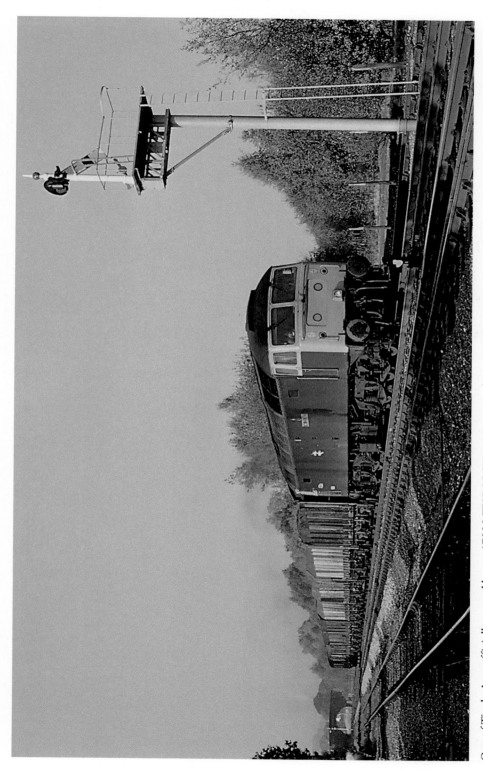

One of Tinsley's unofficially named locos, 47323 *THE JOSTINOT*, passes through Weston Rhyn on 12 October 1990 with empty timber wagons that have just been unloaded at the nearby paper mills at Chirk.

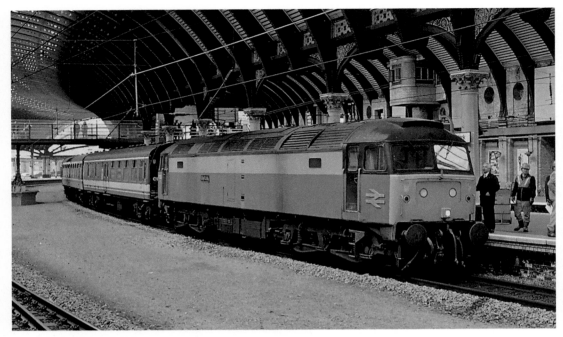

Standing in York station platform nine, 47333 *CIVIL LINK*, is unusual power for a TransPennine service that includes a Network Southeast coach. August 1991.

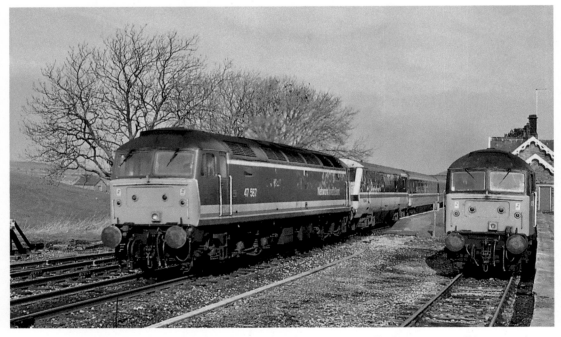

When trains were diverted from the WCML over the S&C, a standby loco was usually stationed at Blea Moor, but on 27 March 1993 47501 *CRAFTSMAN* was at Kirkby Stephen station. It is seen here being passed by 47587 heading a Glasgow to Euston Service.

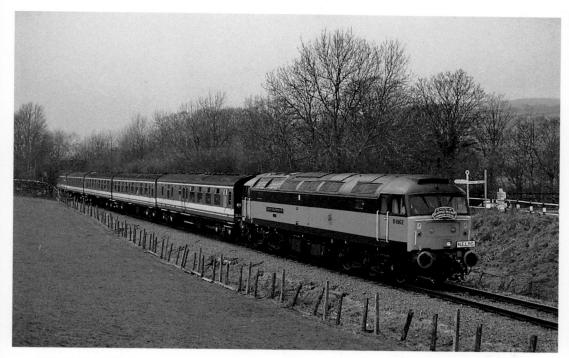

47833 (D1962) *CAPTAIN PETER MAINSTY* is seen here near Stanhope on the Weardale Railway special train that ran from Darlington to Eastgate on 28 March 1993.

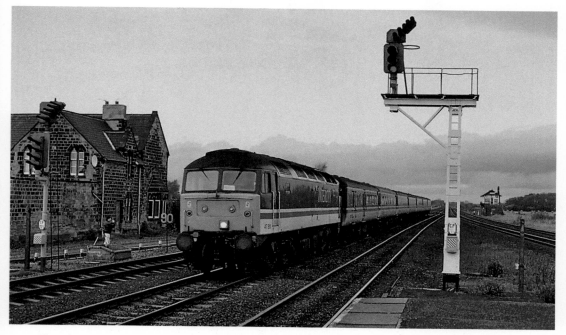

Church Fenton station on 5 June 1993, with 47811 making for Leeds with a CrossCountry service. The buildings on the left are the remains of the 1848 rebuilding of the station.

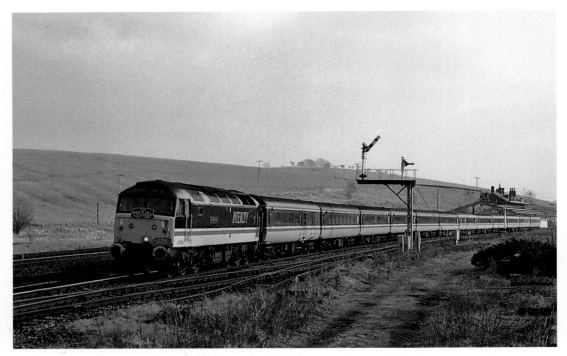

47823 *SS GREAT BRITAIN* passes Hellifield with the Peaks and Fells Explorer Railtour on 12 February 1994.

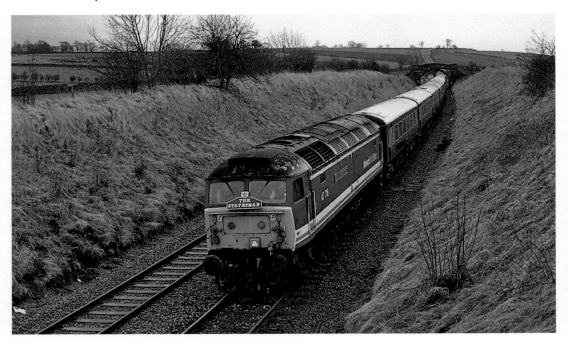

47716 *DUKE OF EDINBURGH AWARD* passes Edenhall as it makes for Carlisle with the The Statesman Railtour on 19 February 1994.

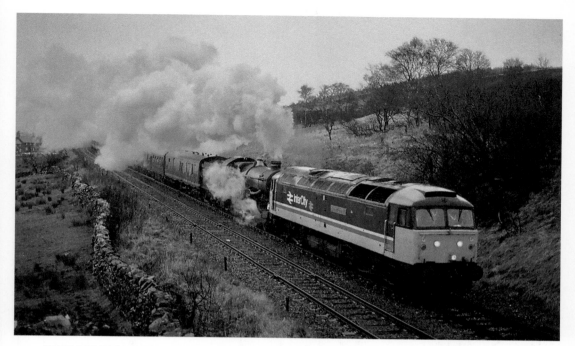

47471 *NORMAN TUNNA GC* and 5029 *NUNNEY CASTLE* depart from Garsdale with the Cumbrian Mountain Express on 12 March 1994. 5029 was having steaming problems due to poor coal.

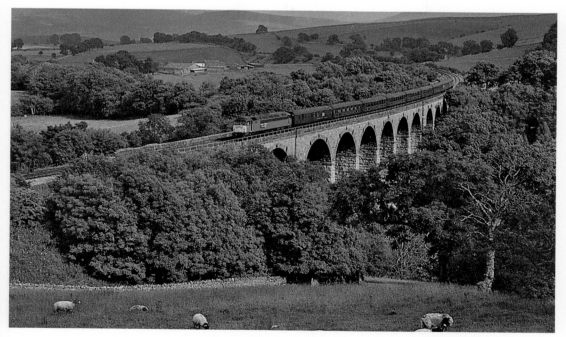

A Class 47 heads the Royal Scotsman luxury train to Carlisle across the 131-foot-high Smardale viaduct on 16 July 1994.

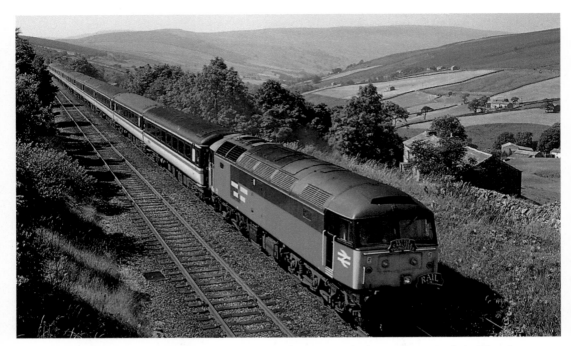

47763 approaches Garsdale station on 30 July 1994 with the Settle & Carlisle Thunderer tour. The passengers have picked the perfect day to travel the famous line and take in the superb scenery.

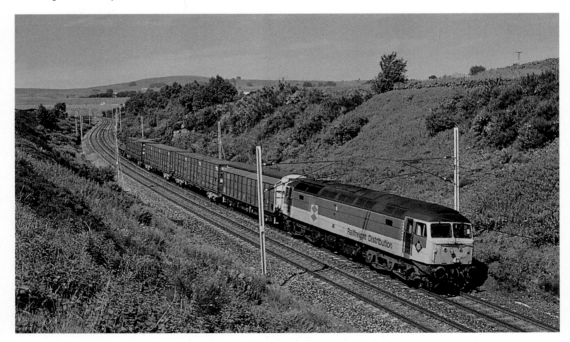

Railfreight Distribution 47307 drifts down the gradient from Shap Summit at Greenholme with a short freight train on 16 July 1996.

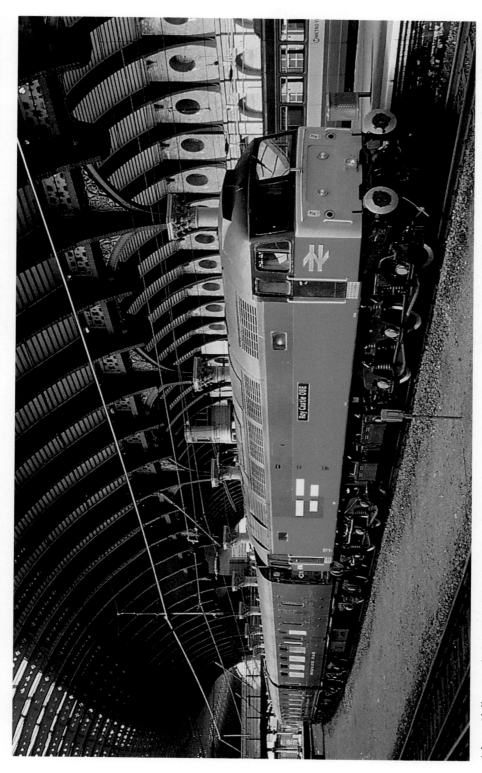

A beautifully turned out 47786 *ROY CASTLE OBE* waits for departure from platform nine at York station with the Royal Scotsman luxury train in June 1995.

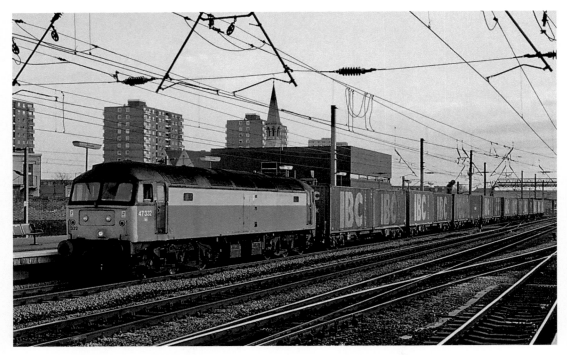

47332 passes through Doncaster station in March 1998 with a short northbound container train.

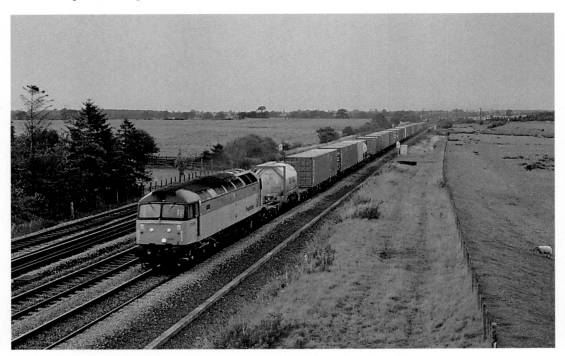

Freightliner 47339 passes Colton Junction with a container train most likely making for Southampton in July 1998.

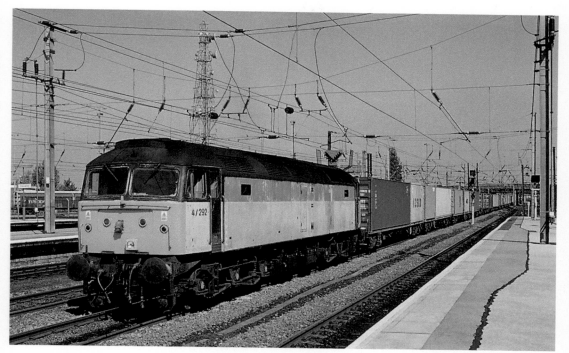

A rather shabby looking 47292 passes through Doncaster station with a container train for Felixstowe on 28 April 1999.

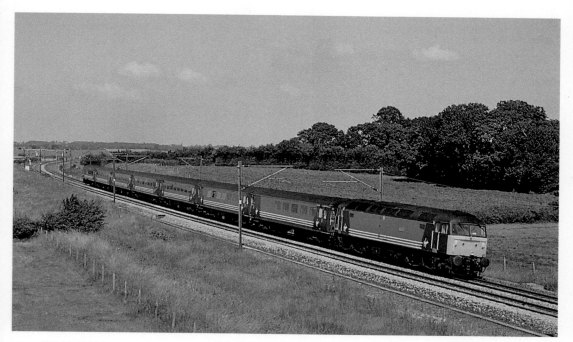

47814 *TOTNES CASTLE* has just passed Colton Junction and heads down the ECML with a Virgin CrossCountry service for Plymouth on 11 July 1999.

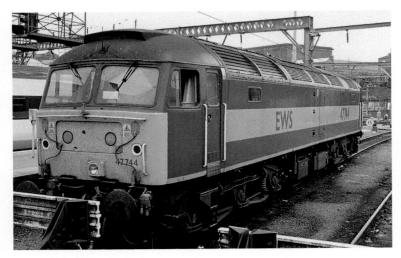

EWS 47744 is the standby loco at Kings Cross on a July day in 2000. This siding disappeared when platform zero was converted from the former taxi road in 2010.

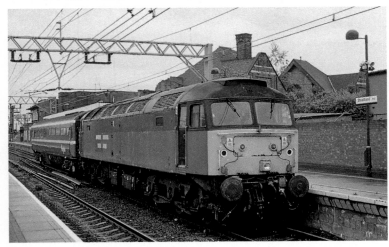

RES 47782 is seen at Stratford station with an Anglia Railways buffet car, which it is taking to Norwich after being overhauled. 4 June 2003.

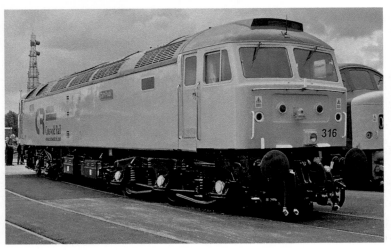

CR 47316 *CAM PEAK* is seen at Doncaster Works at the display held to mark the 150th Anniversary of the works on 26 July 2003. Cotswold Rail was a short-lived company that was founded in 2000 to hire out locos and rolling stock, but was wound up in 2010.

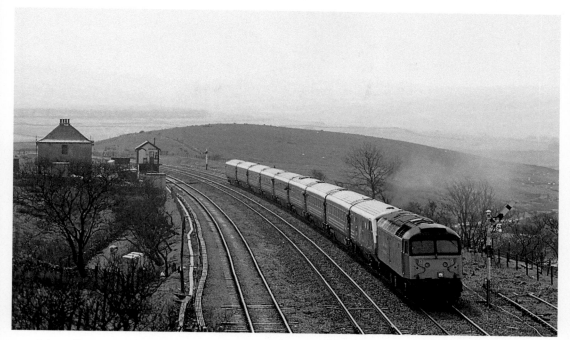

More diversions of WCML trains over the Settle & Carlisle took place on 23 March 2002 and the next three pictures were taken at Blea Moor of northbound trains. First is an unidentified RES Class 47 climbing away from Ribblehead viaduct with a Virgin Euston to Glasgow service.

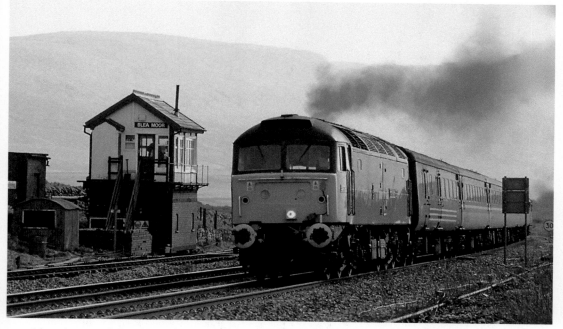

Next is one of the EWS Class 47s that were used on royal trains. 47799 *PRINCE HENRY* passes Blea Moor box with a Virgin CrossCountry service.

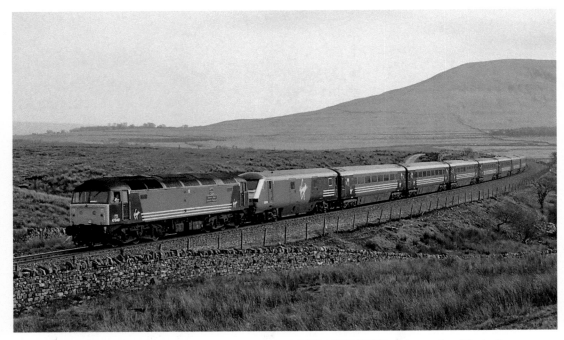

Finally, 47848 *NEWTON ABBOT FESTIVAL OF TRANSPORT* heads another Virgin Euston to Glasgow train towards Carlisle.

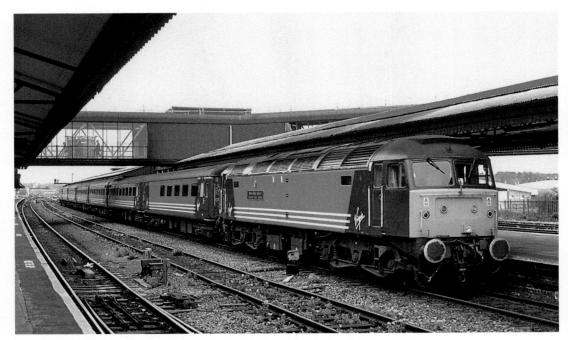

47828 *SEVERN VALLEY RAILWAY* has just arrived at Reading with a Virgin CrossCountry service from Bournemouth, and will run round its train and then set off for Newcastle. 17 April 2002.

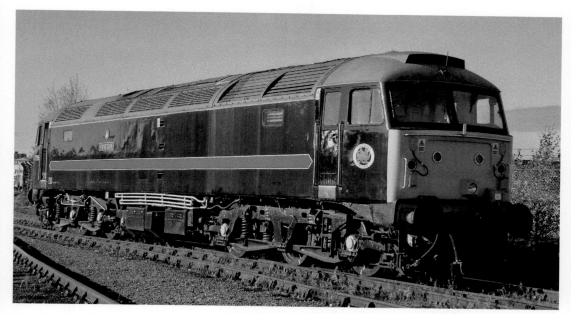

Another short-lived company was Fragonset, which hired out locos and other various related activities. It merged with another company, Merlin Rail, to form FM Rail, but went into administration in 2006. One of their locos, 47715 *POSEIDON*, is seen at an exhibition held at the National Railway Museum in York on 13 November 2004. It is now at Harry Needle's Railroad Company at Worksop.

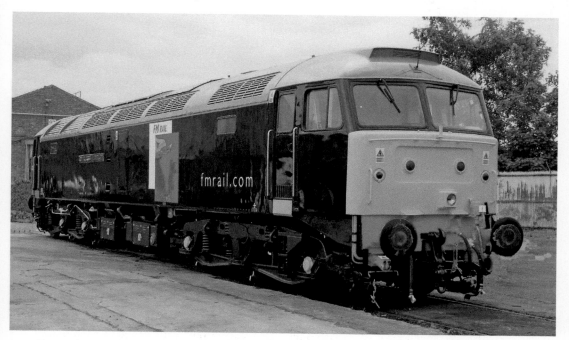

FM Rail 47832 *DRIVER TOM CLARK OBE* is fresh from overhaul, and is seen taking part in the Crewe Works Open Day held on 10 September 2005.

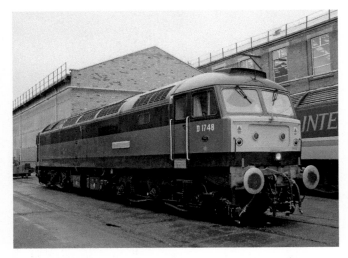

The following three pictures were taken at the Crewe Works Open Day on 10 September 2005. First, 47815 (D1748) *GREAT WESTERN* is looking very smart in its original two-tone green livery. This loco was given the Tops number of 47155 in 1974 and can be seen in this guise on page 47.

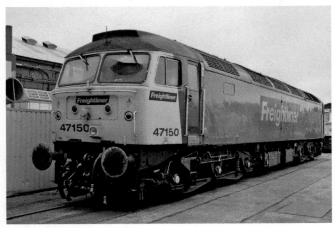

47150 was at this time one of the Freightliner fleet, but was withdrawn in 2008 and scrapped by T.J. Thompson in Stockton.

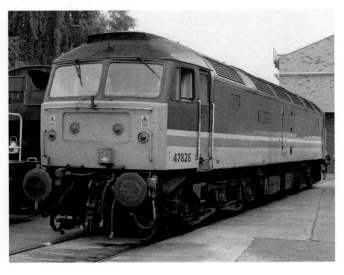

47826 *SPRINGBURN* seen here soon after its purchase by West Coast Railways still in InterCity livery, but was soon repainted into their maroon colours and lost its name at that time.

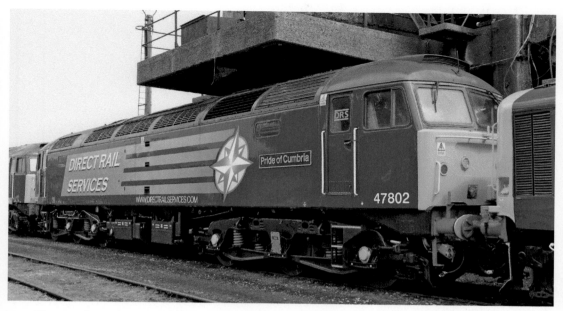

The next four pictures were taken at the Open Day held by WCRC 26 July 2008 at their main workshops and depot in the former steam MPD at Carnforth in Lancashire. First, 47802 *PRIDE OF CUMBRIA* is standing by the coaling plant at Carnforth. It is seen here in DRS livery, but in 2014 was sold to WCRC and is currently part of their fleet.

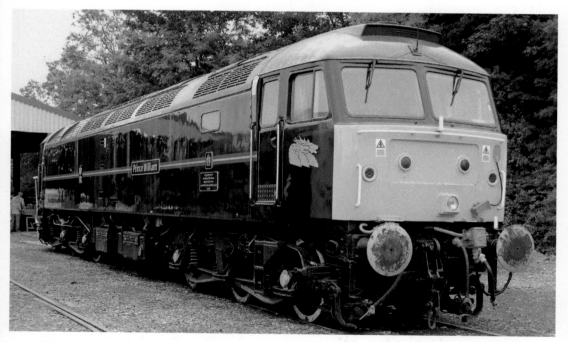

47798 *PRINCE WILLIAM* in Royal train livery. As part of the EWS fleet, 47798 and 47799 were specially painted to haul the Royal trains and remained on these duties until 2004. 47798 is now part of the National Collection and can be seen in the NRM at York.

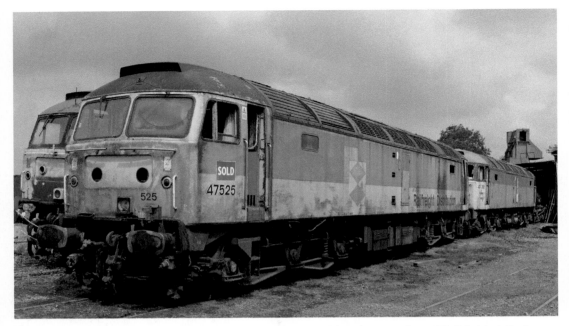

47525 looks to be waiting the scrapman, but wears a sold sticker – as does 47368 behind. Both locos were sold for their spare parts, but 47525 was eventually scrapped by European Metal Recycling at Kingsbury in August 2010.

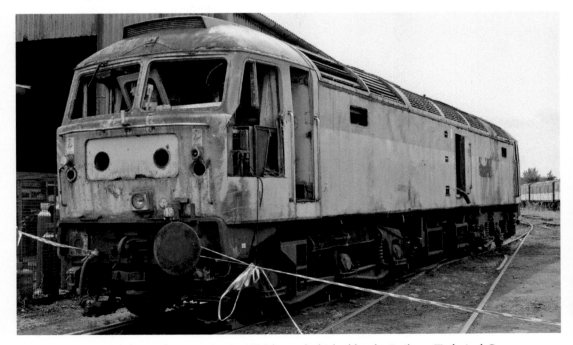

47972 was withdrawn from service in 1989 but refurbished by the Railway Technical Centre at Derby, renumbered 97545 and used to haul test trains. It was eventually scrapped at C.F. Booth Rotherham in 2010.

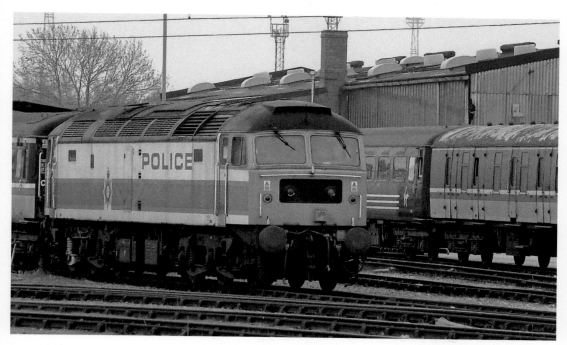

47829 is seen at Crewe diesel depot on 22 April 2006 It was painted in the BT Police livery in 2002 and as part of the Virgin fleet it worked CrossCountry services until put into store in September 2008. It was eventually cut up by C.F. Booth at Rotherham in 2013.

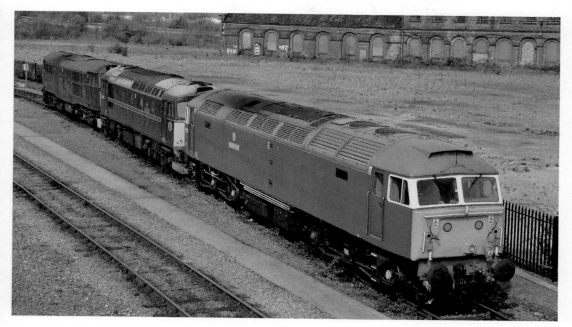

47709 *DIONYSOS* seen here alongside Derby station when in the ownership of FM Rail. It is in their blue livery for working Blue Pullman trains. The other two locos are 33002 and 31190, which were also owned by FM Rail at the time. 22 April 2006.

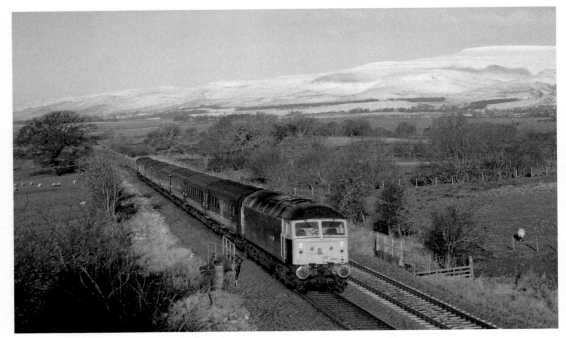

47805 *TALISMAN* is on the rear of Compass Tours Festive Fellsman Railtour, passing Keld and heading towards Carlisle on 6 December 2008 with the snow-covered North Pennines as a beautiful backdrop. 47815 was the front loco.

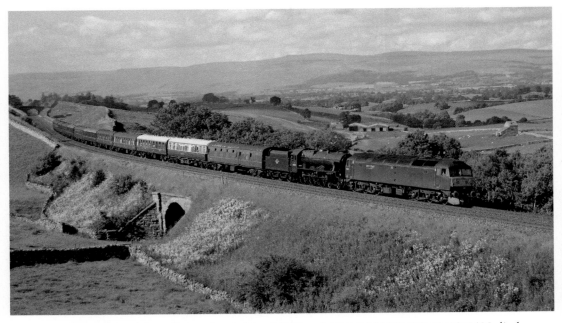

In perfect weather, The Fellsman headed by 47760 and 46115 *SCOTS GUARDSMAN* climbs past Birkett Common, with the Eden Valley as a glorious backdrop on 27 July 2011. 47760 was on the train as the very dry conditions presented a fire hazard.

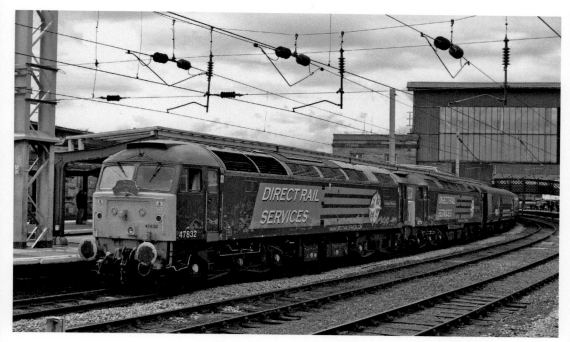

DRS Class 47s 47832 *SOLWAY PRINCESS* and 47712 *PRIDE OF CARLISLE* wait to leave Carlisle with the Pathfinders' Lakes and Borders Explorer tour for its journey back to Eastleigh on 16 July 2011.

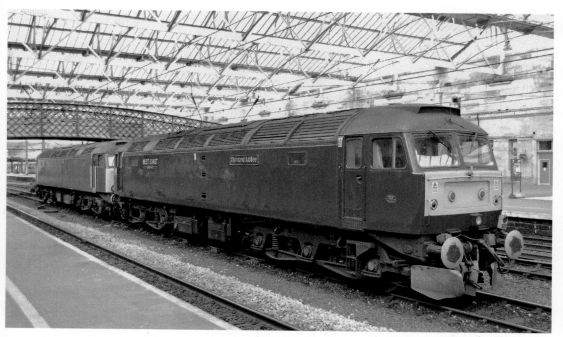

WCR 47854 *DIAMOND JUBILEE* stands on one of the middle roads at Carlisle station with 57316 on 16 July 2013.

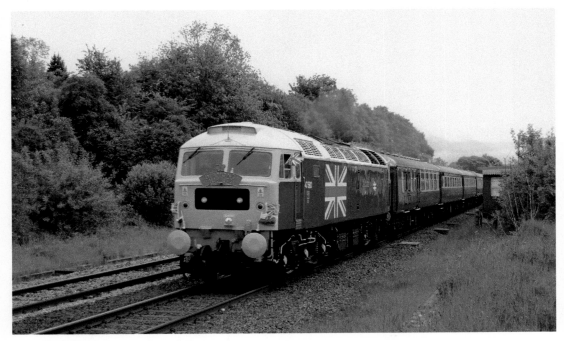

The Stratford 47 Group-owned Class 47580 *COUNTY OF ESSEX*, complete with much
Union Jack waving, speeds through Appleby station towards Carlisle with the Settle & Carlisle
Statesman tour on 2 June 2012.

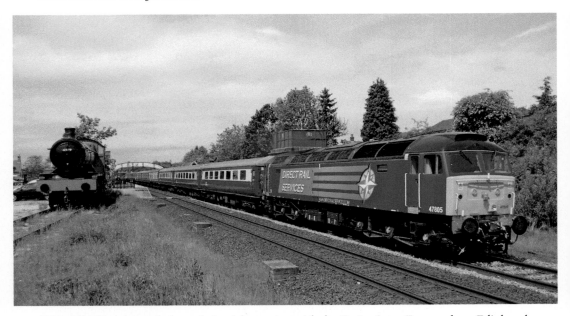

DRS 47805 heads south through Appleby station with the Cruise Saver Express from Edinburgh
to Southampton Docks with 47802 on the rear on 2 June 2012. On the left is 4979 *WOOTON
HALL*, owned by the Furness Railway Trust, which was taken to the Ribble Steam Railway in
October 2014 for restoration.

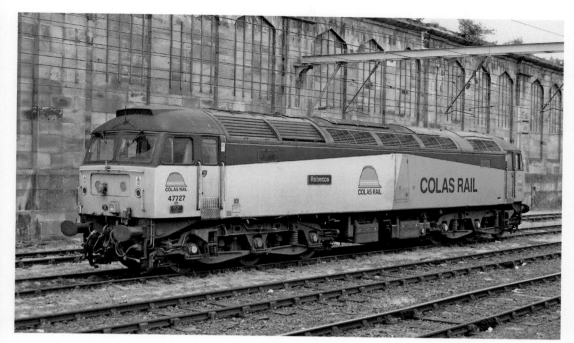

Colas Rail 47727 *REBECCA* is on the back road awaiting its next duty at Carlisle station on 13 June 2014.

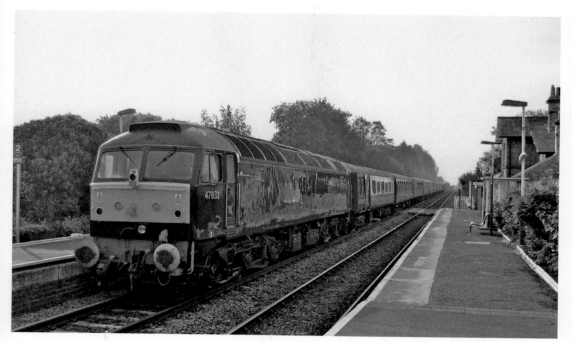

WCR 47832 is on the rear of empty stock returning to Carnforth on 5 October 2014 after working the previous day's special train from Bridlington to Blackpool and return. Taken at Hutton Cranswick station on 5 October 2014.

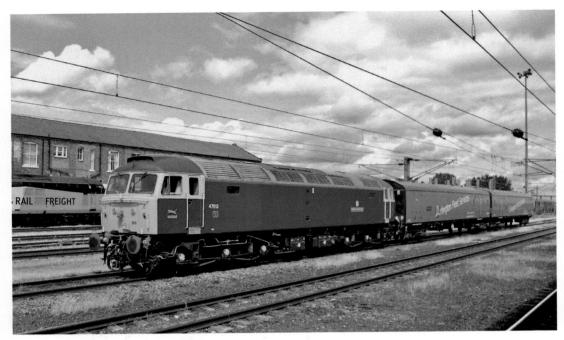

Rail Operations Group's 47815 *GREAT WESTERN* is waiting to head south at Doncaster with two Arlington Fleet Services vehicles on 7 July 2015.

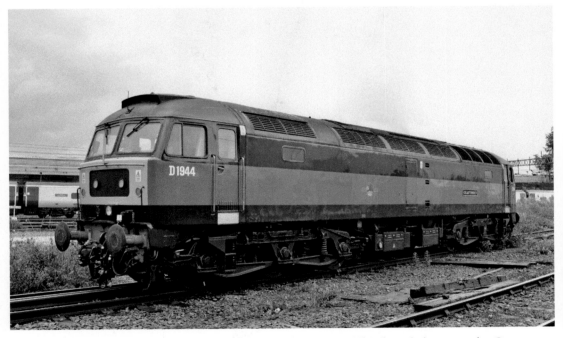

D1944 *CRAFTSMAN* at Crewe Open Day 8 June 2019. This loco belongs to the Crewe Diesel Preservation Group and will return to main line working as part of a deal with Loco Services Limited.

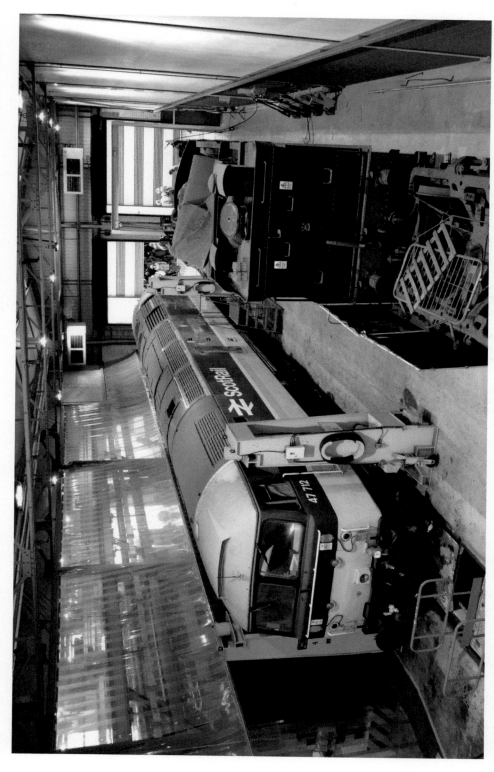

47712 in Scotrail livery is inside the Locomotive Services Workshop at Crewe on 8 June 2019, nearing the end of its overhaul.

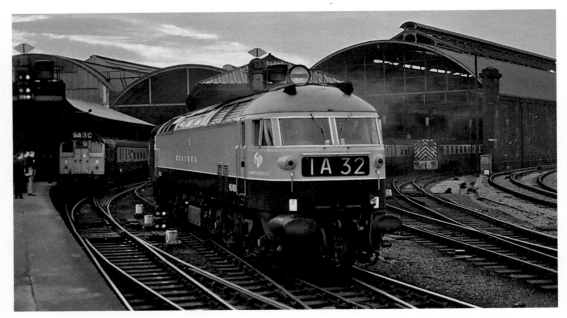

Above and below: Two pictures of the *KESTREL* 4000 hp experimental loco, departing from Newcastle with the 17.00 to Kings Cross on 20 October 1969. Although not strictly within the remit of this book, *KESTREL* was fitted with a Sulzer 16LVA24 engine and was built by Brush Traction at Loughborough, so is included as it proved to be the final development of the BR Sulzer type 4 locos. *KESTREL* was sold to Russia in 1971 and used for experimental purposes, but is presumed to have been scrapped.

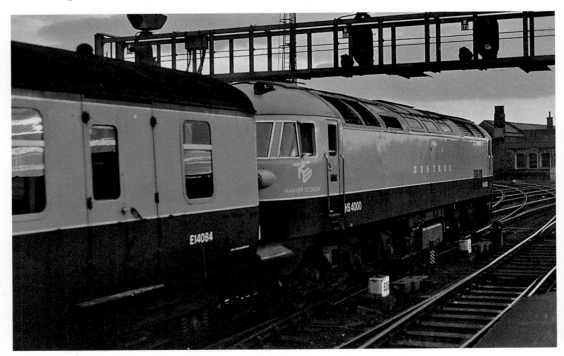

UNDER A YELLOW SUN

A NOVEL BY

CLARK KENT

PROMETHEUS MODERN BOOKS

LONDON ✦ METROPOLIS ✦ SYDNEY ✦ TOKYO

For my parents,
Jonathan and Martha,
whose love and support
gave me my real strength.

Portions of this novel appeared in The Daily Planet
Sunday Magazine, The Smallville Enterprise Press,
and Pacific Monthly.

Library of Congress Cataloguing-in-Publication Data

Kent, Clark. 193&
Under a yellow sun.

I. Title
PMB3&64. F33G6 1993 813'.&4 88-
19466
ISBN 1-56389-109-3

Manufactured in Canada

10 9 8 7 6 5 4 3 2 1

*It's only those who do nothing
that make no mistakes, I suppose.*
JOSEPH CONRAD

Ossie Winters was surprised to find only one man waiting for him at
Toranado field forty minutes ago. *One man.* The Navy must have faith
in this hotshot, he guessed, or maybe they didn't want anyone else for
this mission.

Distant behind tinted glasses, his passenger hadn't said much of
anything since climbing aboard the Ferris Kestrel, the finest helicopter
Star City ever made, to Winter's way of thinking. To tell the truth,
Winters appreciated the lack of conversation. He was piloting the
Kestrel straight into hurricane Joshua, which had shifted south and was
heading for the northwest side of Corto Maltese.

A C-141 transport owned by Caribbean Wind had scratched an engine
and gone down in the Atlantic, a hundred miles north of Ossie's landing
field. Someone in the Corto Maltese senate called the U.S. embassy and
requested aid. The plane carried primarily produce, but this flight also
carried Juan Dalgallo, the Nobel Prize-winning poet, a national treasure,
the voice and conscience of the island nation.

Ossie's Kestrel bounced against the increasing force of the wind. He
hummed to himself, acutely aware that if they went down, there'd be no
one coming for them.

His passenger spotted the downed C-141 before Ossie did, pointing
through the rain-spattered windshield of the copter. It took a full minute
before Ossie could make out the plane's tail, bobbing up and down in the
violent surf. This guy has great vision, he thought.

"This is your game," Ossie told his passenger. "Ready."

His passenger nodded as he unhooked his safety belt.

"You gotta do this fast. We don't have a lot of time. We get this
wrong, you fly home yourself."

"If I have to."

His silent passenger spotted the downed plane before Winters did, pointing through the 'copter's rain-spattered windshield.

It took a full minute before Winters could make out the plane's tail, bobbing up and down in the violent surf.

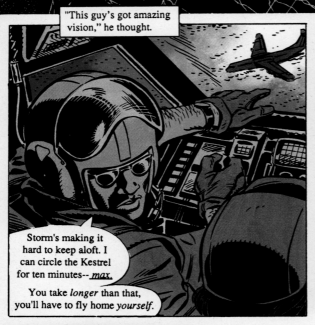

"This guy's got amazing vision," he thought.

Storm's making it hard to keep aloft. I can circle the Kestrel for ten minutes-- *max.*

You take *longer* than that, you'll have to fly home *yourself.*

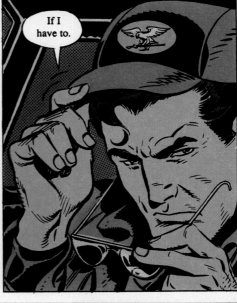

If I have to.

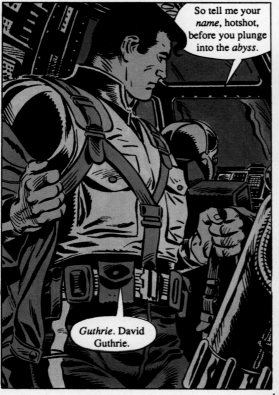

So tell me your *name*, hotshot, before you plunge into the *abyss.*

Guthrie. David Guthrie.

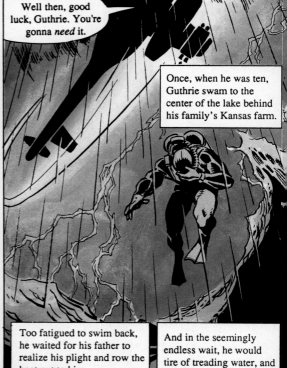

Well then, good luck, Guthrie. You're gonna *need* it.

Once, when he was ten, Guthrie swam to the center of the lake behind his family's Kansas farm.

Too fatigued to swim back, he waited for his father to realize his plight and row the boat out to him.

And in the seemingly endless wait, he would tire of treading water, and sink below the surface--

4

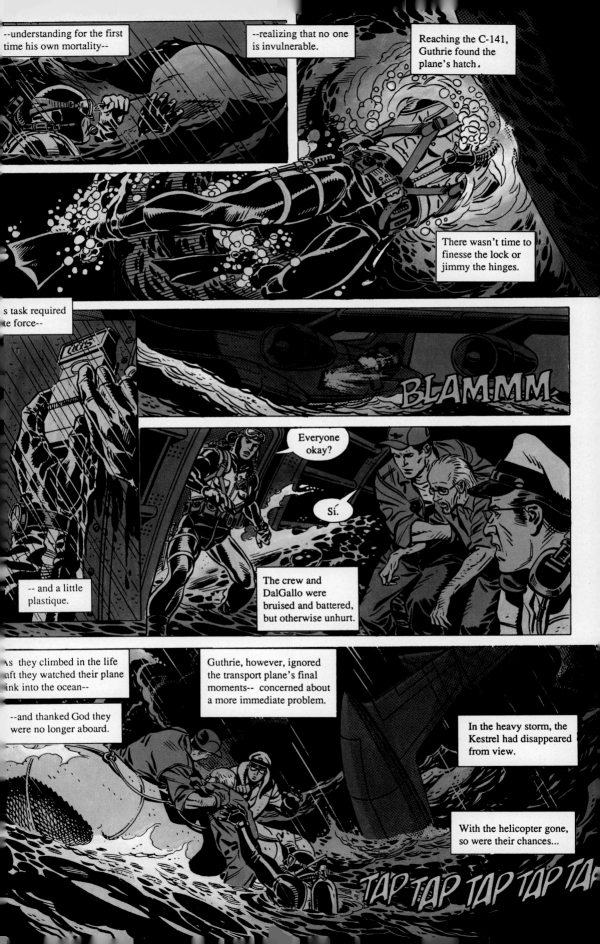

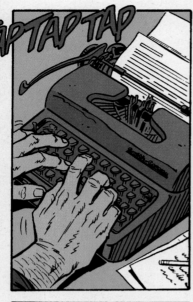

TAP TAP TAP

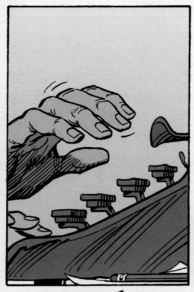

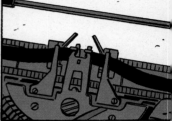

and DalGallo were bruised

limbed in the life raft the
cean and thanked God they
owever, ignored the transp
a more immediate problem.
ppeared from view. With t
es of survival.

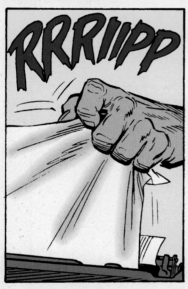

RRRIIPP

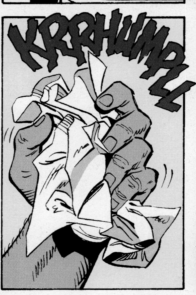

KRRHUMPLL

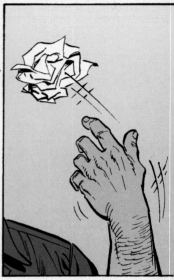

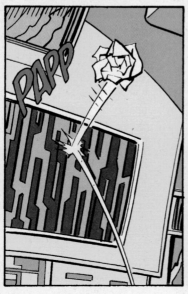

PAPP

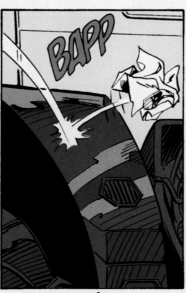

BAPP

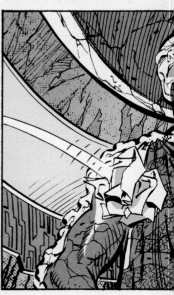

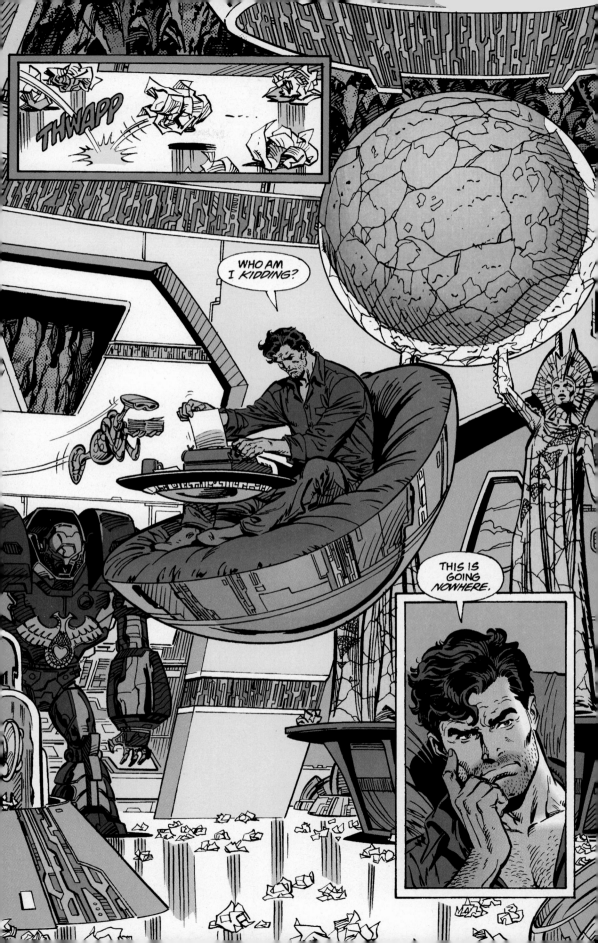

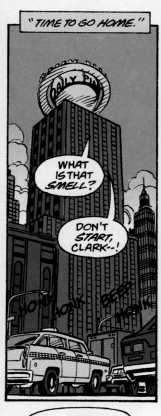

"TIME TO GO HOME."

WHAT IS THAT SMELL?

DON'T START, CLARK--!

HONK HONK BEEP HONK

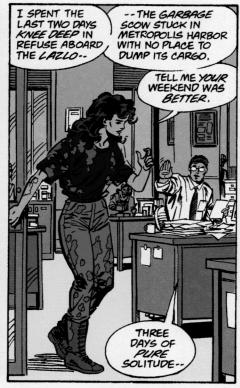

I SPENT THE LAST TWO DAYS KNEE DEEP IN REFUSE ABOARD THE LAZLO--

--THE GARBAGE SCOW STUCK IN METROPOLIS HARBOR WITH NO PLACE TO DUMP ITS CARGO.

TELL ME YOUR WEEKEND WAS BETTER.

THREE DAYS OF PURE SOLITUDE--

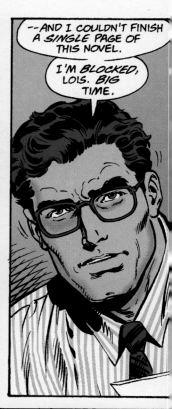

--AND I COULDN'T FINISH A SINGLE PAGE OF THIS NOVEL.

I'M BLOCKED, LOIS. BIG TIME.

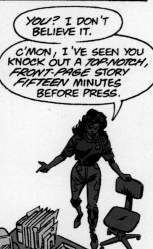

YOU? I DON'T BELIEVE IT.

C'MON, I'VE SEEN YOU KNOCK OUT A TOP-NOTCH, FRONT-PAGE STORY FIFTEEN MINUTES BEFORE PRESS.

NEWS, NOT FICTION. REPORTING THE FACTS IS A LOT EASIER THAN MAKING THEM UP.

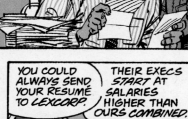

PLUS, SINCE I BOUGHT MY APARTMENT, I OWE EVERYBODY. LOOK AT ALL THESE BILLS.

EVEN WITH THE FINAL PAYMENT FOR THE NOVEL, I'M IN DEBT THROUGH NEXT YEAR.

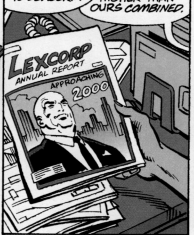

YOU COULD ALWAYS SEND YOUR RESUMÉ TO LEXCORP.

THEIR EXECS START AT SALARIES HIGHER THAN OURS COMBINED.

LEXCORP ANNUAL REPORT APPROACHING 2000

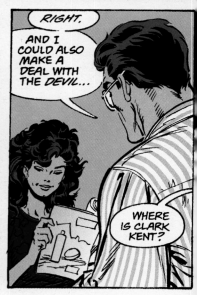

RIGHT, AND I COULD ALSO MAKE A DEAL WITH THE DEVIL...

WHERE IS CLARK KENT?

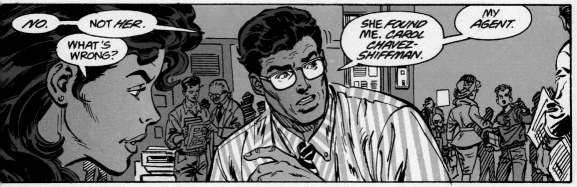

NO.

NOT HER.

WHAT'S WRONG?

SHE FOUND ME. CAROL CHAVEZ-SHIFFMAN.

MY AGENT.

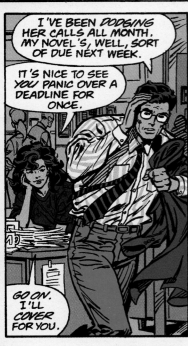

I'VE BEEN DODGING HER CALLS ALL MONTH. MY NOVEL'S, WELL, SORT OF DUE NEXT WEEK.

IT'S NICE TO SEE YOU PANIC OVER A DEADLINE FOR ONCE.

GO ON. I'LL COVER FOR YOU.

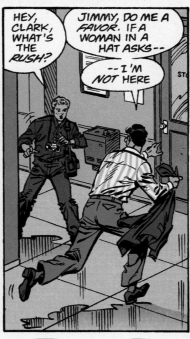

HEY, CLARK, WHAT'S THE RUSH?

JIMMY, DO ME A FAVOR. IF A WOMAN IN A HAT ASKS--

--I'M NOT HERE

STO

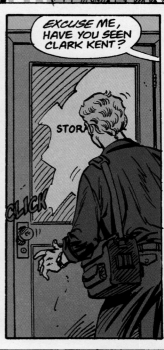

EXCUSE ME, HAVE YOU SEEN CLARK KENT?

STORA

CLICK

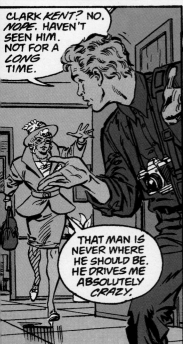

CLARK KENT? NO. NOPE. HAVEN'T SEEN HIM. NOT FOR A LONG TIME.

THAT MAN IS NEVER WHERE HE SHOULD BE. HE DRIVES ME ABSOLUTELY CRAZY.

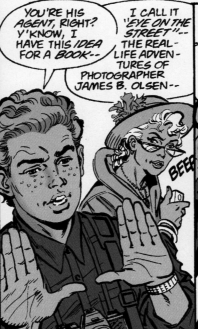

YOU'RE HIS AGENT, RIGHT? Y'KNOW, I HAVE THIS IDEA FOR A BOOK--

I CALL IT "EYE ON THE STREET"-- THE REAL- LIFE ADVEN- TURES OF PHOTOGRAPHER JAMES B. OLSEN--

BEEP

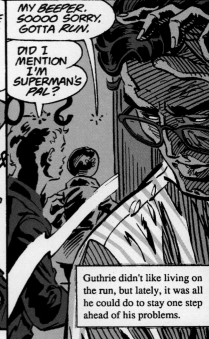

MY BEEPER. SOOOO SORRY. GOTTA RUN.

DID I MENTION I'M SUPERMAN'S PAL?

Guthrie didn't like living on the run, but lately, it was all he could do to stay one step ahead of his problems.

9

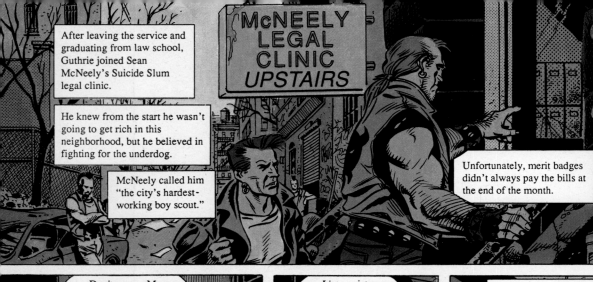

After leaving the service and graduating from law school, Guthrie joined Sean McNeely's Suicide Slum legal clinic.

He knew from the start he wasn't going to get rich in this neighborhood, but he believed in fighting for the underdog.

McNeely called him "the city's hardest-working boy scout."

McNEELY LEGAL CLINIC UPSTAIRS

Unfortunately, merit badges didn't always pay the bills at the end of the month.

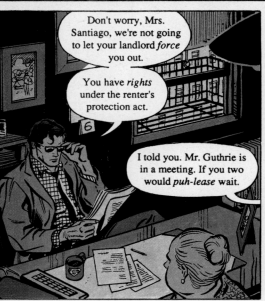

Don't worry, Mrs. Santiago, we're not going to let your landlord *force* you out.

You have *rights* under the renter's protection act.

I told you. Mr. Guthrie is in a meeting. If you two would *puh-lease* wait.

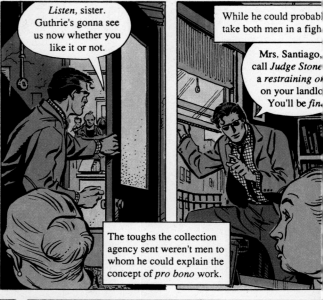

Listen, sister. Guthrie's gonna see us now whether you like it or not.

The toughs the collection agency sent weren't men to whom he could explain the concept of *pro bono* work.

While he could probabl take both men in a figh

Mrs. Santiago, call *Judge Stone* a *restraining o* on your landlo You'll be *fin*

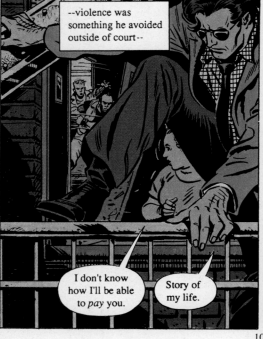

--violence was something he avoided outside of court--

I don't know how I'll be able to *pay* you.

Story of my life.

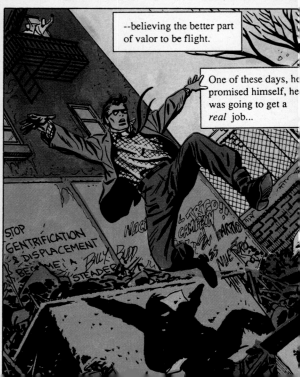

--believing the better part of valor to be flight.

One of these days, he promised himself, he was going to get a *real* job...

STOP GENTRIFICATION & DISPLACEMENT

...one without the noise and aggravation.

BAKROOMM

REPEAT--FIRE-FIGHT AT CORNER OF VERNE AND CHASE-- SUSPECTS ARE ARMED AND DANGEROUS--

REQUEST BACKUP.

LOTS OF BACKUP.

BOYS, DON'T YOU THINK YOU'VE DONE ENOUGH DAMAGE?

UH OH. IT'S THE S-MAN! WHAT NOW, K?

ZZZUNNDDTT

KRSH

STOP ACTING LIKE A SCARED EIGHT-YEAR-OLD AND WASTE HIM!

BOOKS

BARGAINS

I'LL TAKE THAT AS A NO.

THREE NINETY-EIGHT?

IT'S BEEN REMAIN-DERED?

BEFORE YOU DO SOMETHING PROFOUNDLY STUPID--

-- CONSIDER SURRENDER AND SAVING EVERYBODY SOME TIME AND GRIEF.

WRONG CHOICE, BUT YOU'LL FIGURE THAT OUT SOON EN --

11

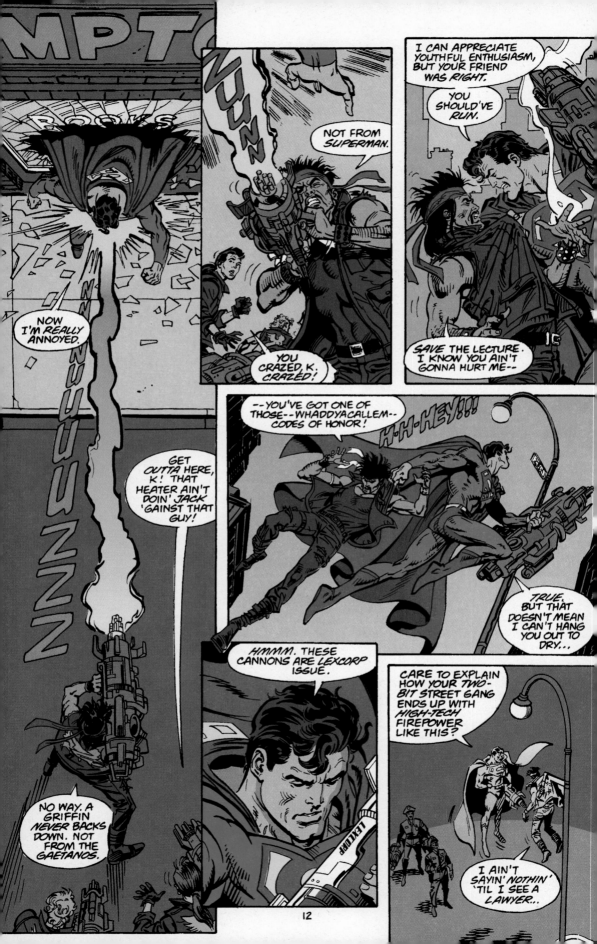

NOW I'M REALLY ANNOYED.

NOT FROM SUPERMAN.

YOU CRAZED, K! CRAZED!

I CAN APPRECIATE YOUTHFUL ENTHUSIASM, BUT YOUR FRIEND WAS RIGHT.

YOU SHOULD'VE RUN.

SAVE THE LECTURE. I KNOW YOU AIN'T GONNA HURT ME--

GET OUTTA HERE, K! THAT HEATER AIN'T DOIN' JACK 'GAINST THAT GUY!

--YOU'VE GOT ONE OF THOSE--WHADDYACALLEM-- CODES OF HONOR!

H-H-HEY!!!

TRUE, BUT THAT DOESN'T MEAN I CAN'T HANG YOU OUT TO DRY...

HMMM. THESE CANNONS ARE LEXCORP ISSUE.

CARE TO EXPLAIN HOW YOUR TWO-BIT STREET GANG ENDS UP WITH HIGH-TECH FIREPOWER LIKE THIS?

NO WAY. A GRIFFIN NEVER BACKS DOWN. NOT FROM THE GAETANOS.

I AIN'T SAYIN' NOTHIN' 'TIL I SEE A LAWYER...

12

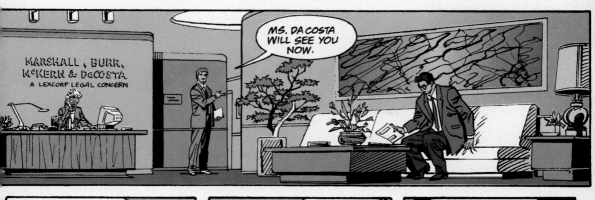

MARSHALL, BURR, McKERN & DeCOSTA
A LEXCORP LEGAL CONCERN

MS. DA COSTA WILL SEE YOU NOW.

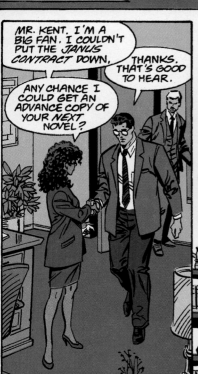

MR. KENT, I'M A BIG FAN. I COULDN'T PUT THE *JANUS CONTRACT* DOWN.

THANKS. THAT'S GOOD TO HEAR.

ANY CHANCE I COULD GET AN ADVANCE COPY OF YOUR *NEXT* NOVEL?

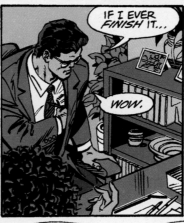

IF I EVER *FINISH* IT...

WOW.

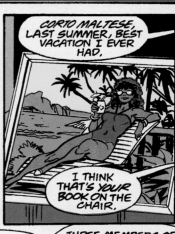

CORTO MALTESE, LAST SUMMER, BEST VACATION I EVER HAD.

I THINK THAT'S *YOUR* BOOK ON THE CHAIR.

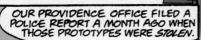

A *VACATION.* THERE'S A FOREIGN CONCEPT.

BUT THAT'S NOT WHY I'M HERE.

THREE MEMBERS OF THE GRIFFIN GANG DESTROYED THE GAETANO SOCIAL CLUB USING LEXCORP WEAPONRY.

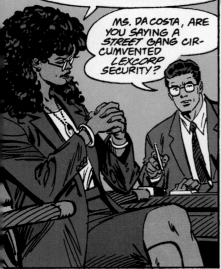

OUR PROVIDENCE OFFICE FILED A POLICE REPORT A MONTH AGO WHEN THOSE PROTOTYPES WERE *STOLEN.*

MS. DA COSTA, ARE YOU SAYING A *STREET* GANG CIRCUMVENTED LEXCORP SECURITY?

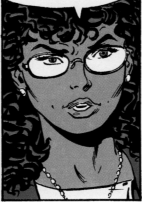

MR. KENT, WHILE LEXCORP *REGRETS* THAT ITS TECHNOLOGY WAS HIJACKED FOR *CRIMINAL* PURPOSES--

--WE *CANNOT* TAKE THE BLAME FOR DAMAGE CAUSED BY SAID CRIMINALS.

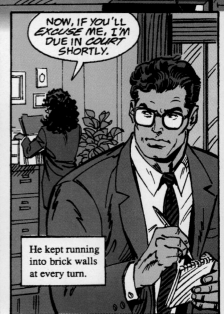

NOW, IF YOU'LL *EXCUSE* ME, I'M DUE IN *COURT* SHORTLY.

He kept running into brick walls at every turn.

13

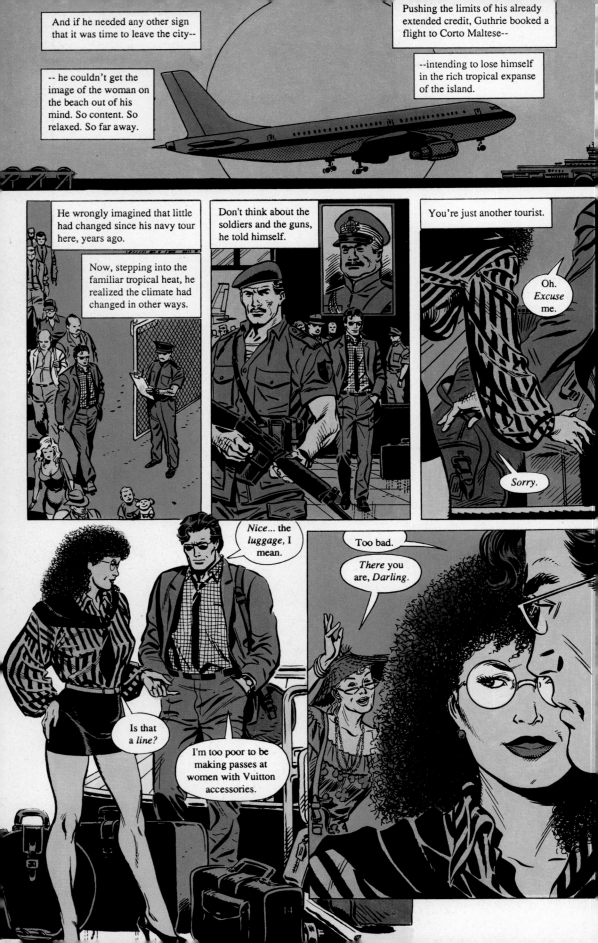

And if he needed any other sign that it was time to leave the city--

Pushing the limits of his already extended credit, Guthrie booked a flight to Corto Maltese--

-- he couldn't get the image of the woman on the beach out of his mind. So content. So relaxed. So far away.

--intending to lose himself in the rich tropical expanse of the island.

He wrongly imagined that little had changed since his navy tour here, years ago.

Now, stepping into the familiar tropical heat, he realized the climate had changed in other ways.

Don't think about the soldiers and the guns, he told himself.

You're just another tourist.

Oh. *Excuse* me.

Sorry.

Nice... the *luggage,* I mean.

Is that a *line?*

I'm too poor to be making passes at women with Vuitton accessories.

Too bad.

There you are, *Darling.*

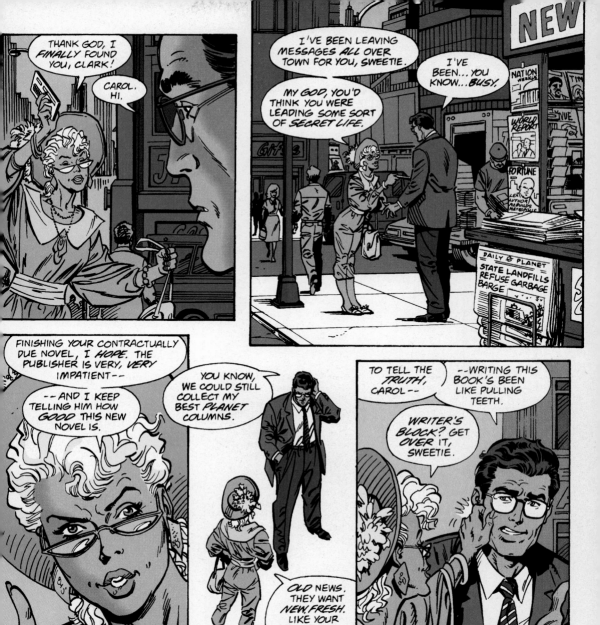

THANK GOD, I *FINALLY* FOUND YOU, CLARK!

CAROL. HI.

I'VE BEEN LEAVING MESSAGES *ALL OVER* TOWN FOR YOU, SWEETIE.

I'VE BEEN... YOU KNOW... *BUSY.*

MY GOD, YOU'D THINK YOU WERE LEADING SOME SORT OF *SECRET LIFE.*

NEW

NATION WEEKLY

WORLD REPORT

FORTUNE

DAILY PLANET
STATE LANDFILLS REFUSE GARBAGE BARGE

FINISHING YOUR CONTRACTUALLY DUE NOVEL, I *HOPE.* THE PUBLISHER IS VERY, *VERY* IMPATIENT--

-- AND I KEEP TELLING HIM HOW *GOOD* THIS NEW NOVEL IS.

YOU KNOW, WE COULD STILL COLLECT MY BEST *PLANET* COLUMNS.

OLD NEWS. THEY WANT *NEW, FRESH.* LIKE YOUR *FIRST* BOOK. ONLY *DIFFERENT.*

TO TELL THE *TRUTH,* CAROL --

--WRITING THIS BOOK'S BEEN LIKE PULLING TEETH.

WRITER'S BLOCK? GET *OVER* IT, SWEETIE.

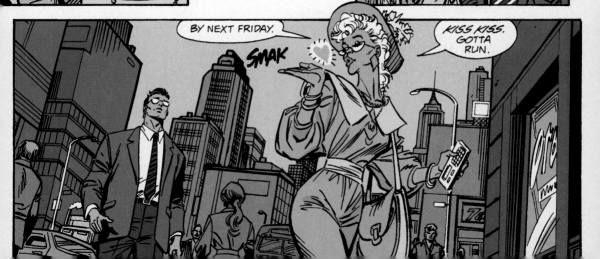

BY NEXT FRIDAY.

SMAK

KISS KISS. GOTTA RUN.

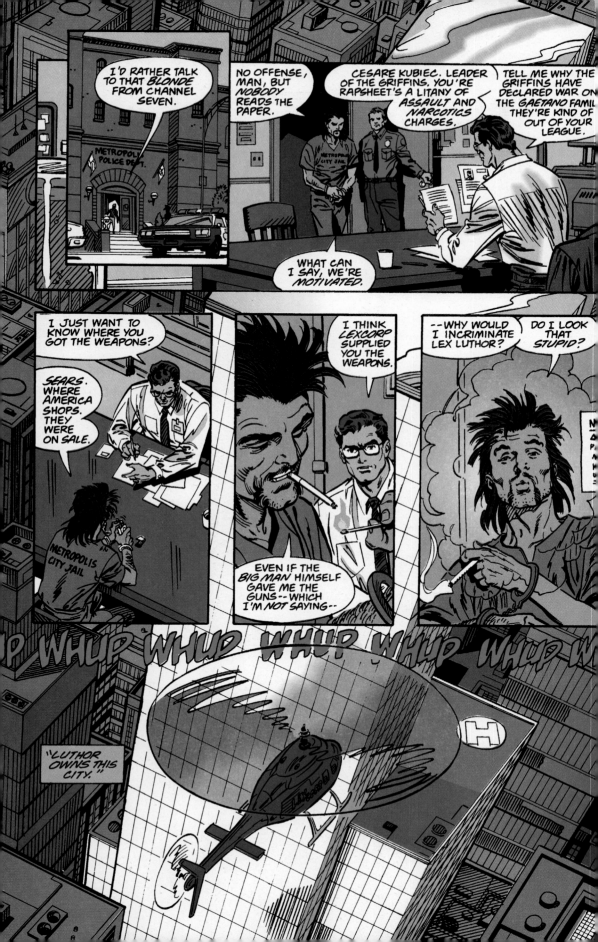

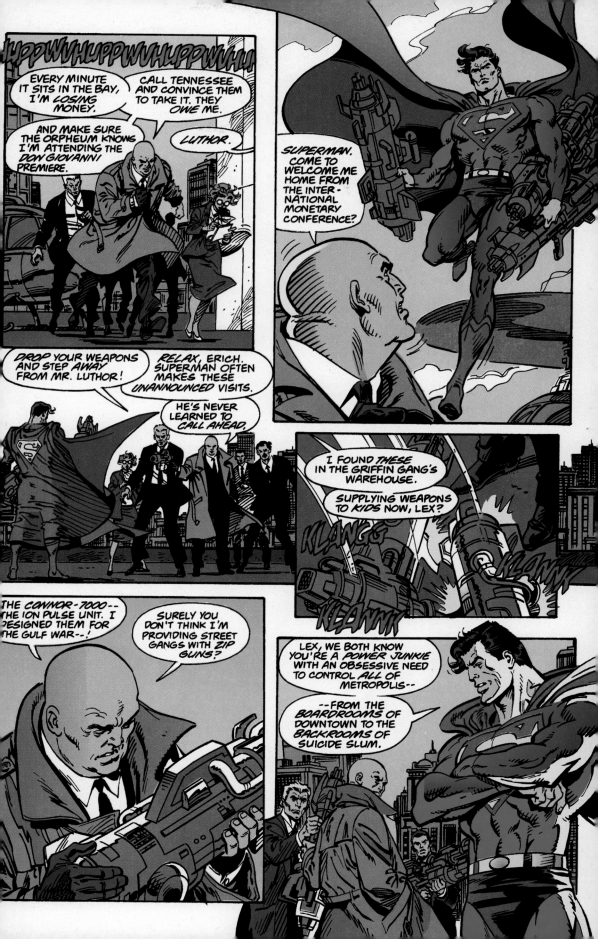

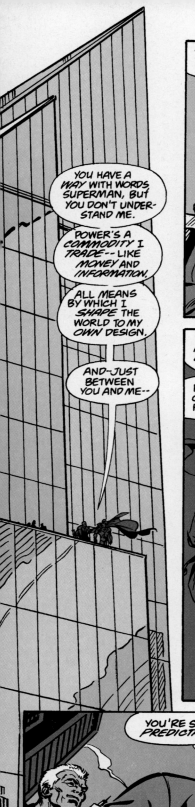
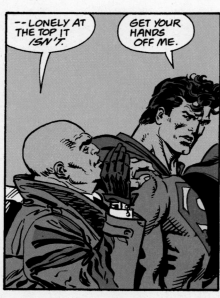
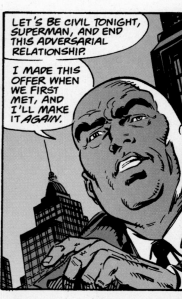
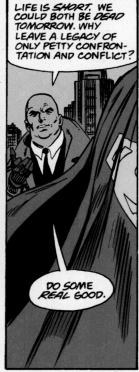
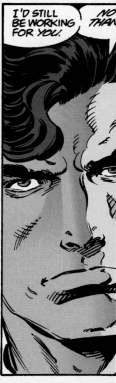
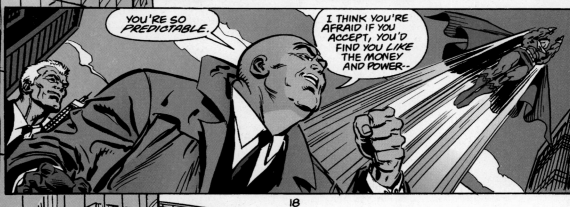

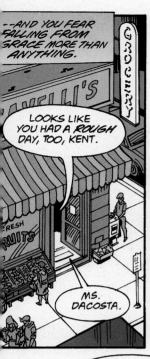

--AND YOU FEAR FALLING FROM GRACE MORE THAN ANYTHING.

LOOKS LIKE YOU HAD A *ROUGH* DAY, TOO, KENT.

MS. DACOSTA.

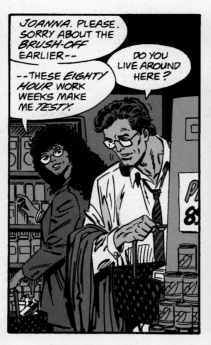

JOANNA. PLEASE. SORRY ABOUT THE *BRUSH-OFF* EARLIER--

--THESE *EIGHTY HOUR* WORK WEEKS MAKE ME *TESTY!*

DO YOU LIVE AROUND HERE?

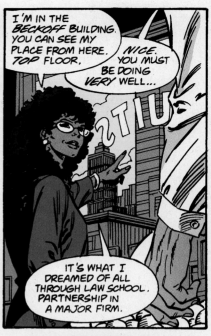

I'M IN THE *BECKOFF* BUILDING. YOU CAN SEE MY PLACE FROM HERE. *TOP* FLOOR.

NICE. YOU MUST BE DOING *VERY* WELL...

IT'S WHAT I DREAMED OF ALL THROUGH LAW SCHOOL. PARTNERSHIP IN A MAJOR FIRM.

TOO BAD THE FIRM'S *LEXCORP.*

YOU GENUINELY *DISLIKE* LUTHOR, DON'T YOU, CLARK?

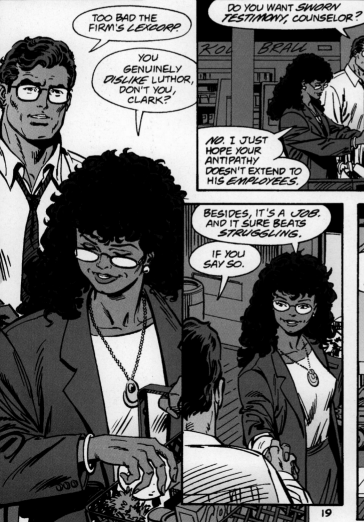

DO YOU WANT *SWORN TESTIMONY*, COUNSELOR?

DAIRY

NO CHECK

NO. I JUST HOPE YOUR ANTIPATHY DOESN'T EXTEND TO HIS *EMPLOYEES.*

BESIDES, IT'S A *JOB.* AND IT SURE BEATS *STRUGGLING.*

IF YOU SAY SO.

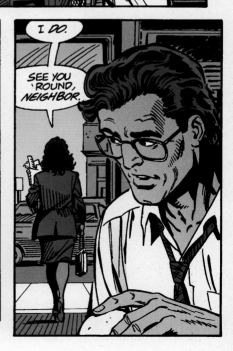

I *DO.*

SEE YOU 'ROUND, NEIGHBOR.

19

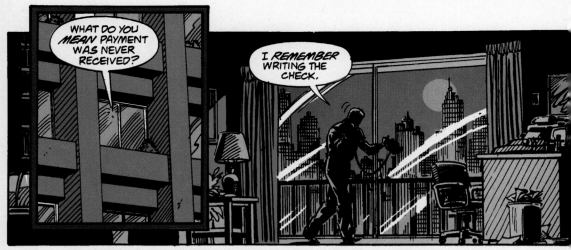

WHAT DO YOU *MEAN* PAYMENT WAS NEVER RECEIVED?

I REMEMBER WRITING THE CHECK.

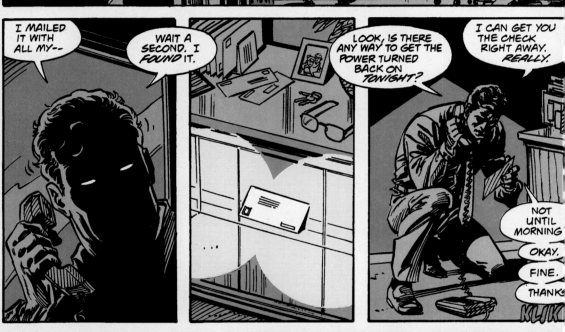

I MAILED IT WITH ALL MY--

WAIT A SECOND. I *FOUND* IT.

LOOK, IS THERE ANY WAY TO GET THE POWER TURNED BACK ON *TONIGHT?*

I CAN GET YOU THE CHECK RIGHT AWAY. *REALLY.*

NOT UNTIL MORNING

OKAY.

FINE.

THANKS

KLIK

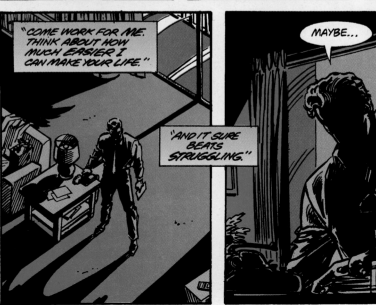

"*COME WORK FOR ME. THINK ABOUT HOW MUCH EASIER I CAN MAKE YOUR LIFE.*"

"*AND IT SURE BEATS STRUGGLING.*"

MAYBE...

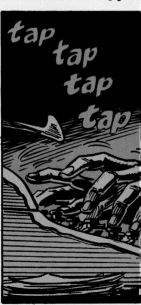

tap tap tap tap

20

Under a yellow sun, floating in its encompassing warmth, he felt reborn.

One life abandoned, taken away by a tropical breeze.

Another begun, washed up on shore with the certainty of the tide.

And, as he floated, suspended between worlds, between lives, he heard the voice of an angel.

You're a hard man to track down, Mr. Guthrie.

An angel with a matching set of Vuitton luggage.

The *desk clerk* at the Hotel Aguila said you had checked out *yesterday*.

Did you sleep on the beach?

Angela Zessoules. I'm here to make you an *offer*.

The only room I can afford. I've *maxxed* all my credit cards.

You have me at a *disadvantage*.

Just for *listening* to the proposition, my employer will pay you *one thousand dollars*.

Interested?

Is that a line?

A thousand bucks. Guthrie knew there would be strings attached.

But with no money, no job, and no home, he didn't have much to lose.

21

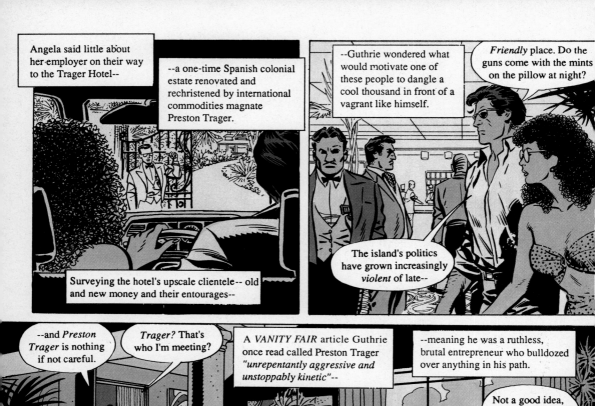

Angela said little about her employer on their way to the Trager Hotel--

--a one-time Spanish colonial estate renovated and rechristened by international commodities magnate Preston Trager.

--Guthrie wondered what would motivate one of these people to dangle a cool thousand in front of a vagrant like himself.

Friendly place. Do the guns come with the mints on the pillow at night?

Surveying the hotel's upscale clientele-- old and new money and their entourages--

The island's politics have grown increasingly *violent* of late--

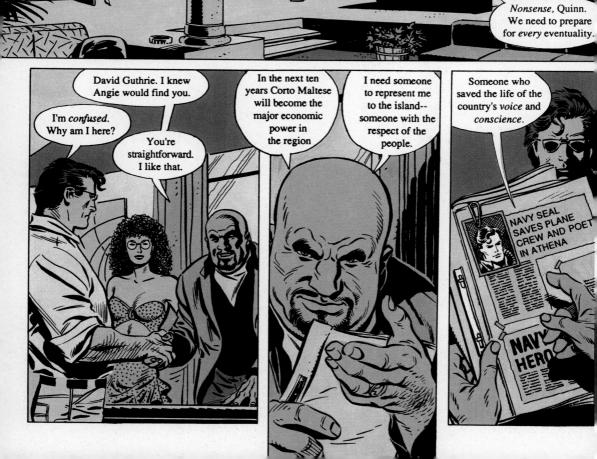

--and *Preston Trager* is nothing if not careful.

Trager? That's who I'm meeting?

A *VANITY FAIR* article Guthrie once read called Preston Trager *"unrepentantly aggressive and unstoppably kinetic"*--

--meaning he was a ruthless, brutal entrepreneur who bulldozed over anything in his path.

Not a good idea, sir. We have a relationship with the General.

Nonsense, Quinn. We need to prepare for *every* eventuality.

David Guthrie. I knew Angie would find you.

I'm *confused*. Why am I here?

You're straightforward. I like that.

In the next ten years Corto Maltese will become the major economic power in the region

I need someone to represent me to the island-- someone with the respect of the people.

Someone who saved the life of the country's *voice* and *conscience*.

NAVY SEAL SAVES PLANE CREW AND POET IN ATHENA

NAVY HERO

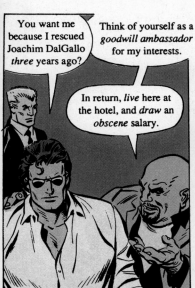

You want me because I rescued Joachim DalGallo *three* years ago?

Think of yourself as a *goodwill ambassador* for my interests.

In return, *live* here at the hotel, and *draw* an *obscene* salary.

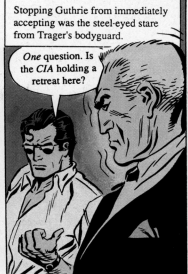

Stopping Guthrie from immediately accepting was the steel-eyed stare from Trager's bodyguard.

One question. Is the *CIA* holding a retreat here?

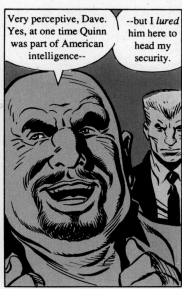

Very perceptive, Dave. Yes, at one time Quinn was part of American intelligence--

--but I *lured* him here to head my security.

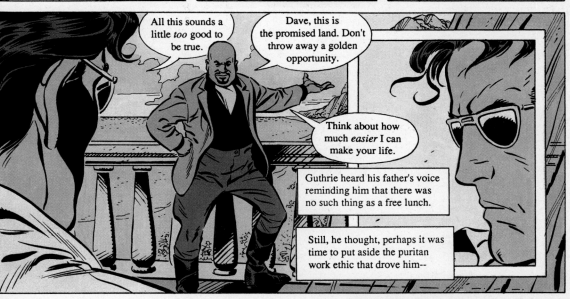

All this sounds a little *too* good to be true.

Dave, this is the promised land. Don't throw away a golden opportunity.

Think about how much *easier* I can make your life.

Guthrie heard his father's voice reminding him that there was no such thing as a free lunch.

Still, he thought, perhaps it was time to put aside the puritan work ethic that drove him--

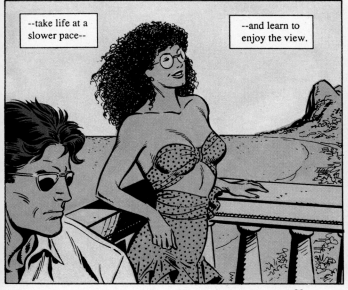

--take life at a slower pace--

--and learn to enjoy the view.

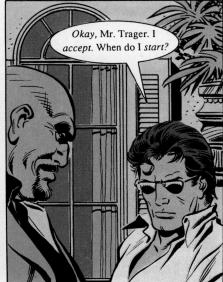

Okay, Mr. Trager. I *accept*. When do I *start*?

23

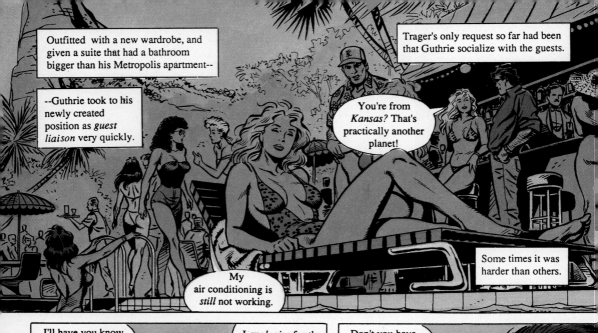

Outfitted with a new wardrobe, and given a suite that had a bathroom bigger than his Metropolis apartment--

--Guthrie took to his newly created position as *guest liaison* very quickly.

Trager's only request so far had been that Guthrie socialize with the guests.

You're from *Kansas?* That's practically another planet!

Some times it was harder than others.

My air conditioning is *still* not working.

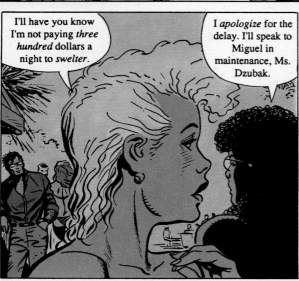

I'll have you know I'm not paying *three hundred* dollars a night to *swelter*.

I *apologize* for the delay. I'll speak to Miguel in maintenance, Ms. Dzubak.

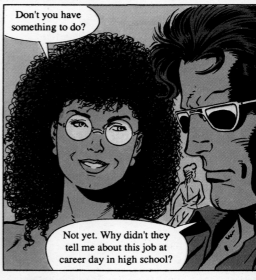

Don't you have something to do?

Not yet. Why didn't they tell me about this job at career day in high school?

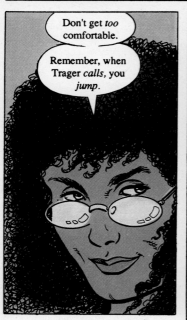

Don't get *too* comfortable.

Remember, when Trager *calls,* you *jump.*

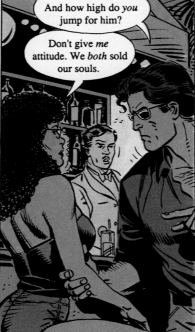

And how high do *you* jump for him?

Don't give *me* attitude. We *both* sold our souls.

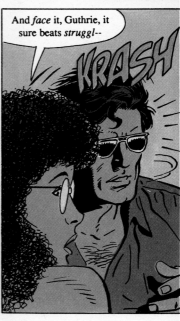

And *face* it, Guthrie, it sure beats *struggl--*

KRASH

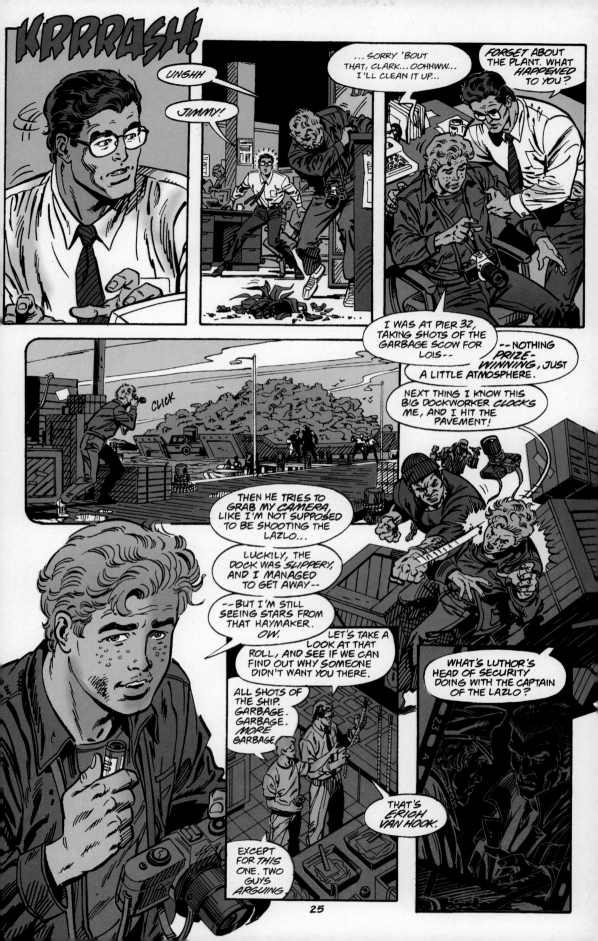

KRRRASH!

UNSHH

JIMMY!

...SORRY 'BOUT THAT, CLARK...OOHHWW... I'LL CLEAN IT UP...

FORGET ABOUT THE PLANT. WHAT HAPPENED TO YOU?

I WAS AT PIER 32, TAKING SHOTS OF THE GARBAGE SCOW FOR LOIS--

--NOTHING PRIZE-WINNING, JUST A LITTLE ATMOSPHERE.

NEXT THING I KNOW THIS BIG DOCKWORKER CLOCKS ME, AND I HIT THE PAVEMENT!

CLICK

THEN HE TRIES TO GRAB MY CAMERA, LIKE I'M NOT SUPPOSED TO BE SHOOTING THE LAZLO...

LUCKILY, THE DOCK WAS SLIPPERY, AND I MANAGED TO GET AWAY--

--BUT I'M STILL SEEING STARS FROM THAT HAYMAKER. OW.

LET'S TAKE A LOOK AT THAT ROLL, AND SEE IF WE CAN FIND OUT WHY SOMEONE DIDN'T WANT YOU THERE.

ALL SHOTS OF THE SHIP. GARBAGE. GARBAGE. MORE GARBAGE.

EXCEPT FOR THIS ONE. TWO GUYS ARGUING

WHAT'S LUTHOR'S HEAD OF SECURITY DOING WITH THE CAPTAIN OF THE LAZLO?

THAT'S ERICH VAN HOOK.

25

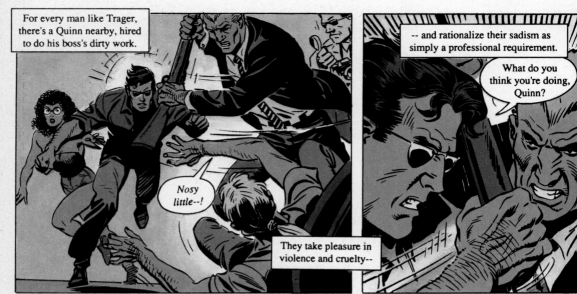

For every man like Trager, there's a Quinn nearby, hired to do his boss's dirty work.

Nosy little--!

They take pleasure in violence and cruelty--

-- and rationalize their sadism as simply a professional requirement.

What do you think you're doing, Quinn?

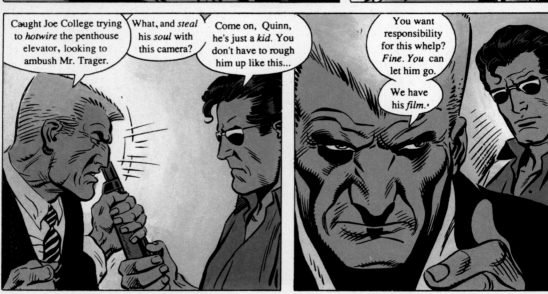

Caught Joe College trying to *hotwire* the penthouse elevator, looking to ambush Mr. Trager.

What, and *steal* his *soul* with this camera?

Come on, Quinn, he's just a *kid*. You don't have to rough him up like this...

You want responsibility for this whelp? *Fine. You* can let him go.

We have his *film.*

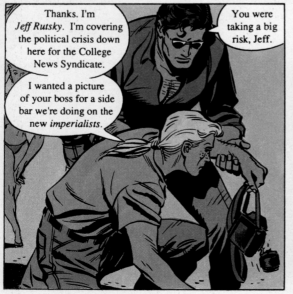

Thanks. I'm *Jeff Rutsky.* I'm covering the political crisis down here for the College News Syndicate.

I wanted a picture of your boss for a side bar we're doing on the new *imperialists.*

You were taking a big risk, Jeff.

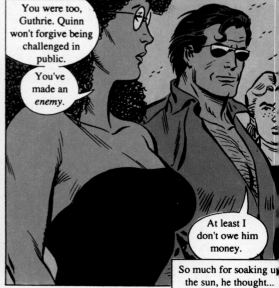

You were too, Guthrie. Quinn won't forgive being challenged in public.

You've made an *enemy.*

At least I don't owe him money.

So much for soaking up the sun, he thought...

26

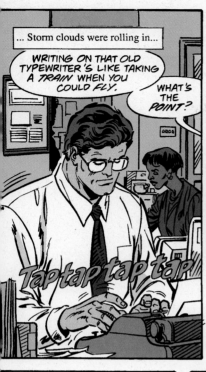

... Storm clouds were rolling in...

WRITING ON THAT OLD TYPEWRITER'S LIKE TAKING A *TRAIN* WHEN YOU COULD *FLY.*

WHAT'S THE *POINT?*

Tap tap tap tap

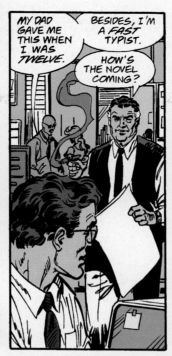

MY DAD GAVE ME THIS WHEN I WAS *TWELVE.*

BESIDES, I'M A *FAST* TYPIST.

HOW'S THE *NOVEL* COMING?

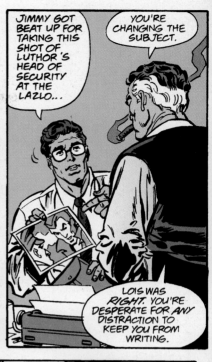

JIMMY GOT BEAT UP FOR TAKING THIS SHOT OF LUTHOR'S HEAD OF SECURITY AT THE LAZLO...

YOU'RE CHANGING THE SUBJECT.

LOIS WAS *RIGHT.* YOU'RE DESPERATE FOR *ANY* DISTRACTION TO KEEP YOU FROM WRITING.

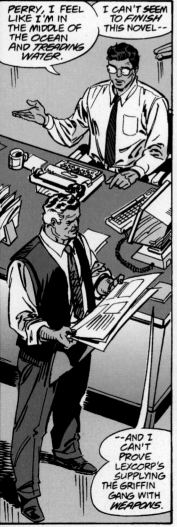

PERRY, I FEEL LIKE I'M IN THE MIDDLE OF THE OCEAN AND *TREADING* WATER.

I CAN'T SEEM TO *FINISH* THIS NOVEL--

--AND I CAN'T PROVE LEXCORP'S SUPPLYING THE GRIFFIN GANG WITH *WEAPONS.*

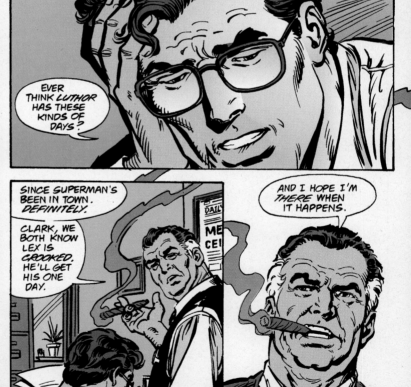

EVER THINK *LUTHOR* HAS THESE KINDS OF DAYS?

SINCE SUPERMAN'S BEEN IN TOWN. *DEFINITELY.*

CLARK, WE BOTH KNOW LEX IS *CROOKED.* HE'LL GET HIS ONE DAY.

AND I HOPE I'M *THERE* WHEN IT HAPPENS.

27

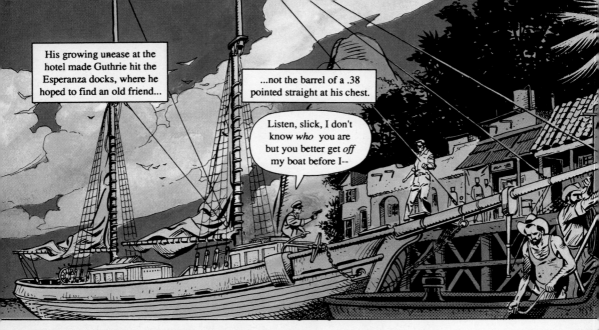

His growing unease at the hotel made Guthrie hit the Esperanza docks, where he hoped to find an old friend...

...not the barrel of a .38 pointed straight at his chest.

Listen, slick, I don't know *who* you are but you better get *off* my boat before I--

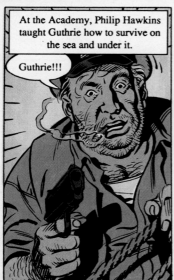

At the Academy, Philip Hawkins taught Guthrie how to survive on the sea and under it.

Guthrie!!!

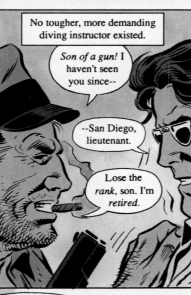

No tougher, more demanding diving instructor existed.

Son of a gun! I haven't seen you since--

--San Diego, lieutenant.

Lose the *rank*, son. I'm *retired*.

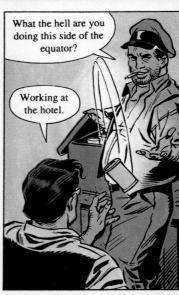

What the hell are you doing this side of the equator?

Working at the hotel.

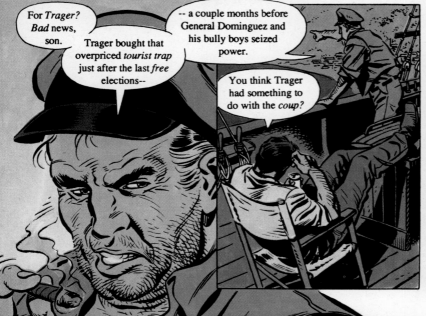

For *Trager? Bad* news, son.

Trager bought that overpriced *tourist trap* just after the last *free* elections--

-- a couple months before General Dominguez and his bully boys seized power.

You think Trager had something to do with the *coup?*

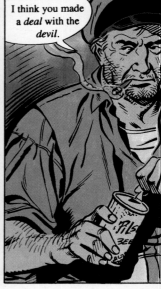

I think you made a *deal* with the *devil.*

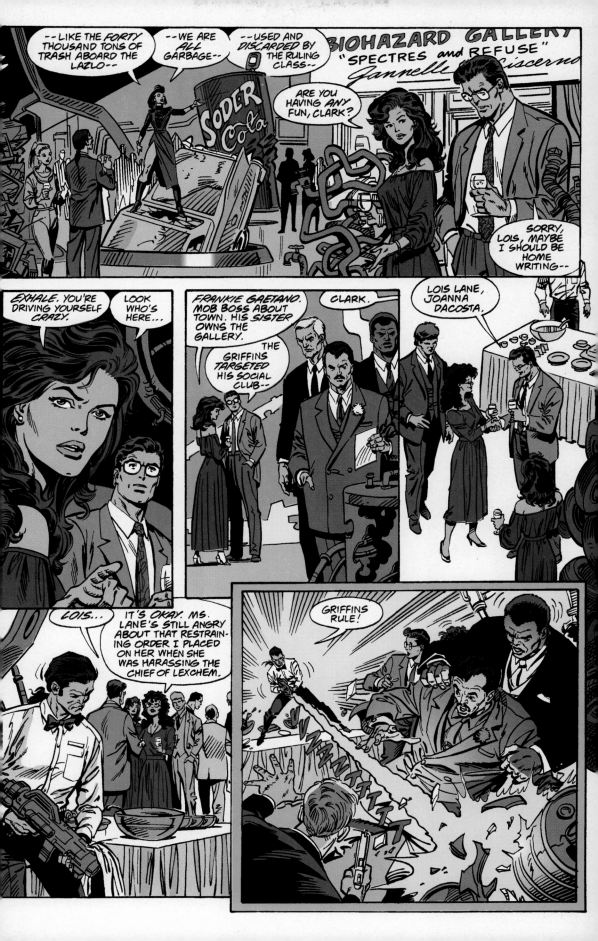

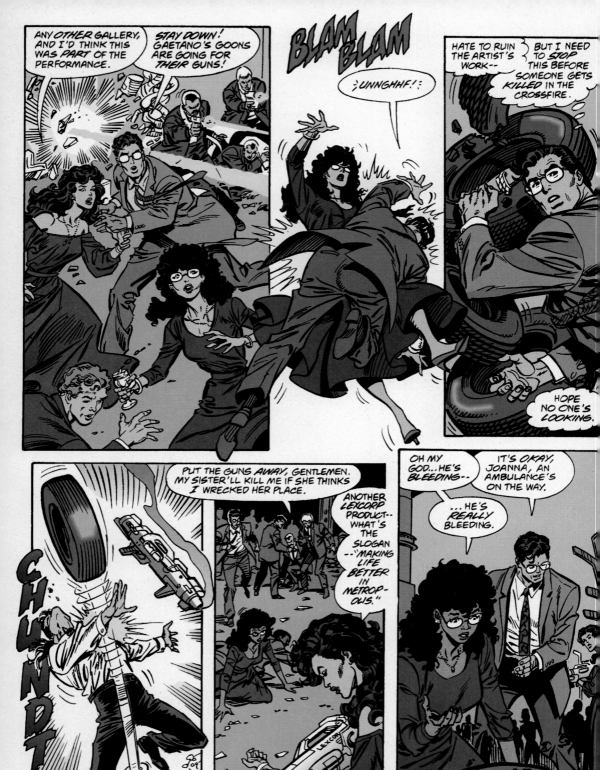

ANY *OTHER* GALLERY, AND I'D THINK THIS WAS *PART* OF THE PERFORMANCE.

STAY DOWN! GAETANO'S GOONS ARE GOING FOR *THEIR* GUNS!

BLAM BLAM

¡UNNGHHF!

HATE TO RUIN THE ARTIST'S WORK--

BUT I NEED TO *STOP* THIS BEFORE SOMEONE GETS *KILLED* IN THE CROSSFIRE.

HOPE NO ONE'S LOOKING.

CHUNDT

PUT THE GUNS *AWAY*, GENTLEMEN. MY SISTER'LL KILL ME IF SHE THINKS *I* WRECKED HER PLACE.

ANOTHER *LEXCORP* PRODUCT-- WHAT'S THE SLOGAN --"MAKING LIFE *BETTER* IN METROP-OLIS."

MAKES YOU PROUD TO BE A COMPANY PLAYER, EH, MS. DaCOSTA?

OH MY GOD...HE'S *BLEEDING*--

IT'S *OKAY,* JOANNA, AN AMBULANCE'S ON THE WAY.

...HE'S *REALLY* BLEEDING.

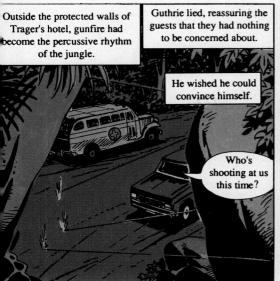

Outside the protected walls of Trager's hotel, gunfire had become the percussive rhythm of the jungle.

Guthrie lied, reassuring the guests that they had nothing to be concerned about.

He wished he could convince himself.

Who's shooting at us this time?

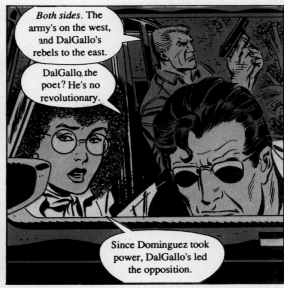

Both sides. The army's on the west, and DalGallo's rebels to the east.

DalGallo, the poet? He's no revolutionary.

Since Dominguez took power, DalGallo's led the opposition.

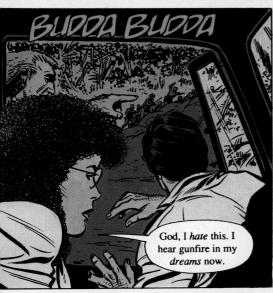

BUDDA BUDDA

God, I *hate* this. I hear gunfire in my *dreams* now.

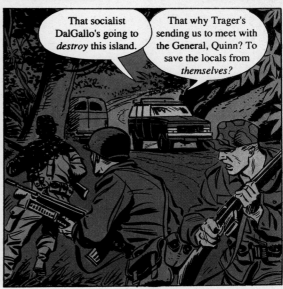

That socialist DalGallo's going to *destroy* this island.

That why Trager's sending us to meet with the General, Quinn? To save the locals from *themselves?*

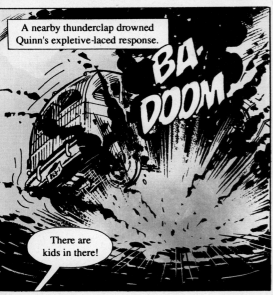

A nearby thunderclap drowned Quinn's expletive-laced response.

BA-DOOM

There are kids in there!

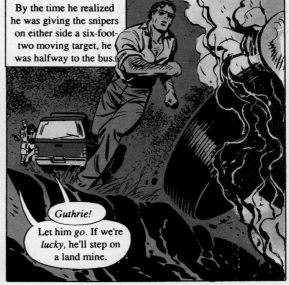

By the time he realized he was giving the snipers on either side a six-foot-two moving target, he was halfway to the bus.

Guthrie!

Let him *go.* If we're *lucky,* he'll step on a land mine.

31

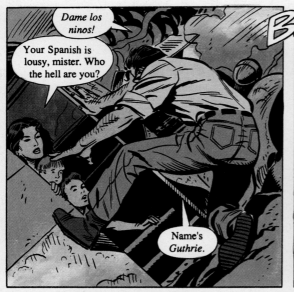

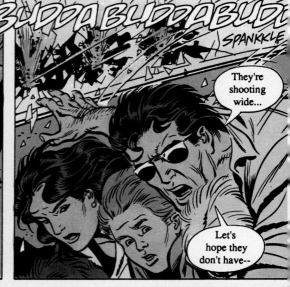

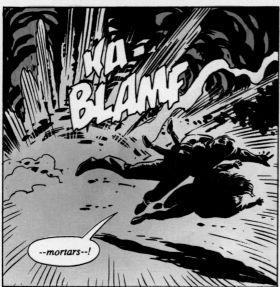

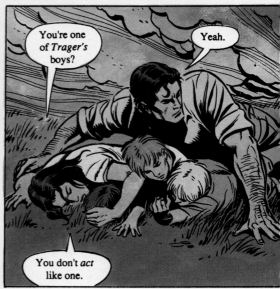

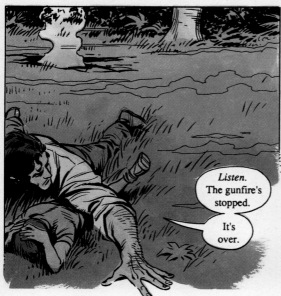

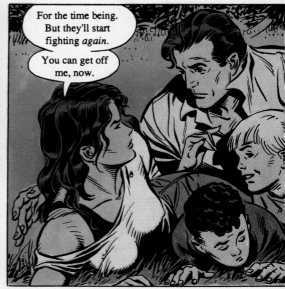

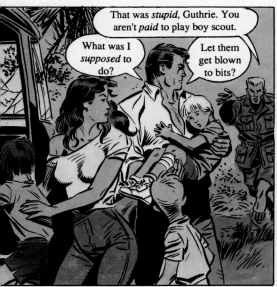

That was *stupid*, Guthrie. You aren't *paid* to play boy scout.

What was I *supposed* to do?

Let them get blown to bits?

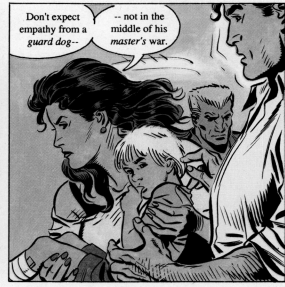

Don't expect empathy from a *guard dog*--

-- not in the middle of his *master's* war.

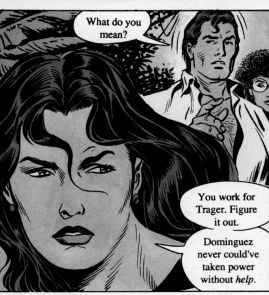

What do you mean?

You work for Trager. Figure it out.

Dominguez never could've taken power without *help*.

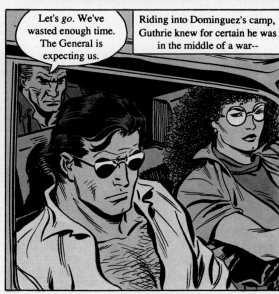

Let's *go*. We've wasted enough time. The General is expecting us.

Riding into Dominguez's camp, Guthrie knew for certain he was in the middle of a war--

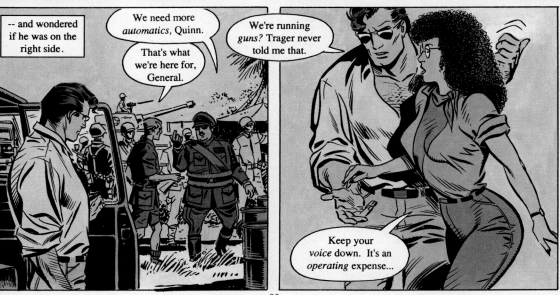

-- and wondered if he was on the right side.

We need more *automatics*, Quinn.

That's what we're here for, General.

We're running *guns*? Trager never told me that.

Keep your *voice* down. It's an *operating* expense...

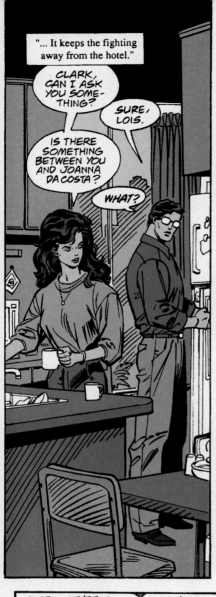

"... It keeps the fighting away from the hotel."

CLARK, CAN I ASK YOU SOMETHING?

SURE, LOIS.

IS THERE SOMETHING BETWEEN YOU AND JOANNA DA COSTA?

WHAT?

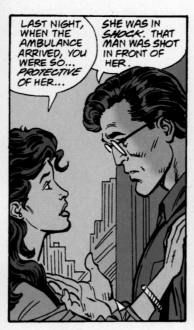

LAST NIGHT, WHEN THE AMBULANCE ARRIVED, YOU WERE SO... PROTECTIVE OF HER...

SHE WAS IN SHOCK. THAT MAN WAS SHOT IN FRONT OF HER.

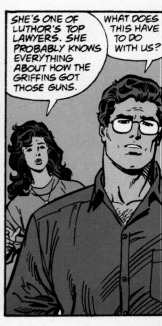

SHE'S ONE OF LUTHOR'S TOP LAWYERS. SHE PROBABLY KNOWS EVERYTHING ABOUT HOW THE GRIFFINS GOT THOSE GUNS.

WHAT DOES THIS HAVE TO DO WITH US?

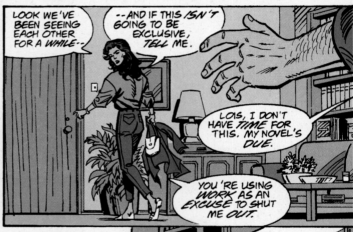

LOOK WE'VE BEEN SEEING EACH OTHER FOR A WHILE--

--AND IF THIS ISN'T GOING TO BE EXCLUSIVE, TELL ME.

LOIS, I DON'T HAVE TIME FOR THIS. MY NOVEL'S DUE.

YOU'RE USING WORK AS AN EXCUSE TO SHUT ME OUT.

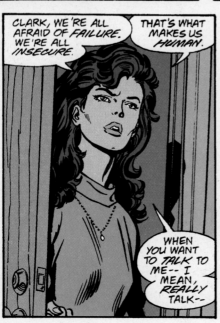

CLARK, WE'RE ALL AFRAID OF FAILURE. WE'RE ALL INSECURE.

THAT'S WHAT MAKES US HUMAN.

WHEN YOU WANT TO TALK TO ME-- I MEAN, REALLY TALK--

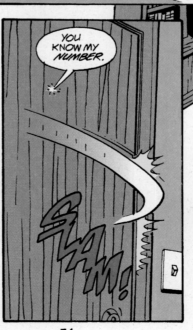

YOU KNOW MY NUMBER.

SLAM!

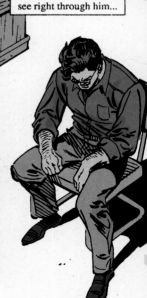

It was like she could see right through him...

34

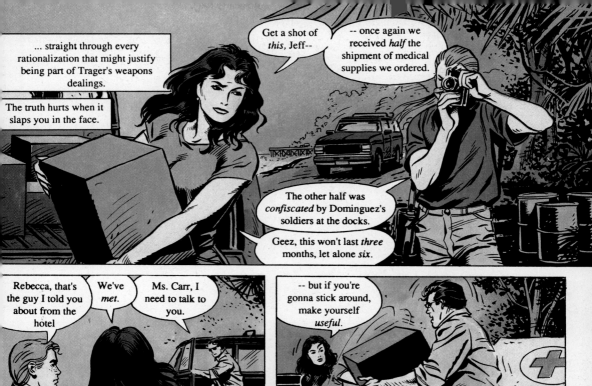

... straight through every rationalization that might justify being part of Trager's weapons dealings.

The truth hurts when it slaps you in the face.

Get a shot of *this*, Jeff--

-- once again we received *half* the shipment of medical supplies we ordered.

The other half was *confiscated* by Dominguez's soldiers at the docks.

Geez, this won't last *three* months, let alone *six*.

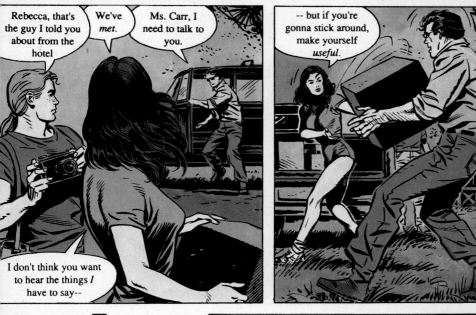

Rebecca, that's the guy I told you about from the hotel

We've *met*.

Ms. Carr, I need to talk to you.

I don't think you want to hear the things *I* have to say--

-- but if you're gonna stick around, make yourself *useful*.

Uumph!

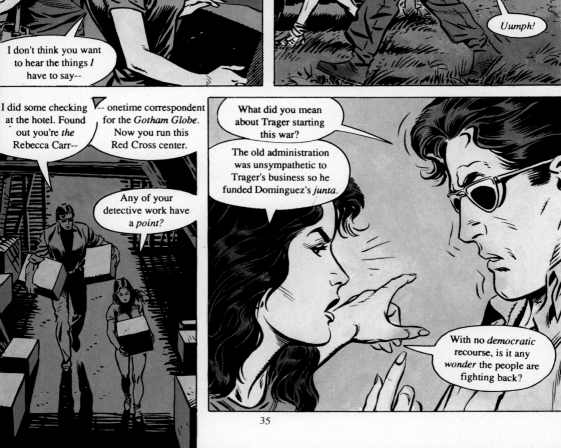

I did some checking at the hotel. Found out you're *the* Rebecca Carr-- -- onetime correspondent for the *Gotham Globe*. Now you run this Red Cross center.

Any of your detective work have a *point*?

What did you mean about Trager starting this war?

The old administration was unsympathetic to Trager's business so he funded Dominguez's *junta*.

With no *democratic* recourse, is it any *wonder* the people are fighting back?

35

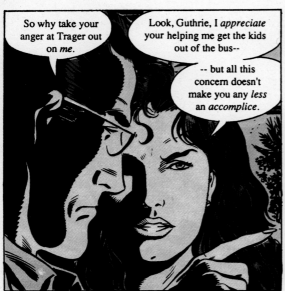

So why take your anger at Trager out on *me*.

Look, Guthrie, I *appreciate* your helping me get the kids out of the bus--

-- but all this concern doesn't make you any *less* an *accomplice*.

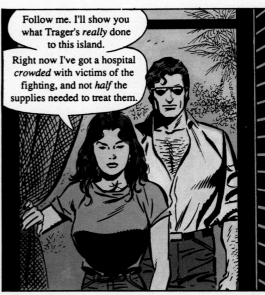

Follow me. I'll show you what Trager's *really* done to this island.

Right now I've got a hospital *crowded* with victims of the fighting, and not *half* the supplies needed to treat them.

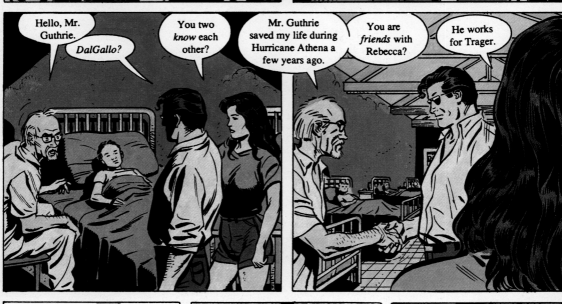

Hello, Mr. Guthrie.

DalGallo?

You two *know* each other?

Mr. Guthrie saved my life during Hurricane Athena a few years ago.

You are *friends* with Rebecca?

He works for Trager.

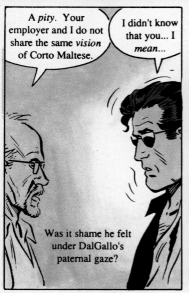

A *pity*. Your employer and I do not share the same *vision* of Corto Maltese.

I didn't know that you... I *mean*...

Was it shame he felt under DalGallo's paternal gaze?

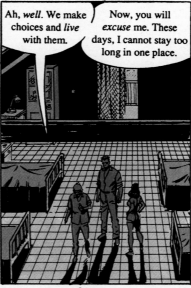

Ah, *well*. We make choices and *live* with them.

Now, you will *excuse* me. These days, I cannot stay too long in one place.

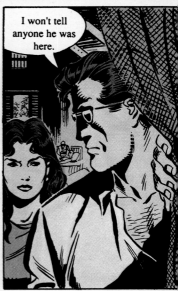

I won't tell anyone he was here.

36

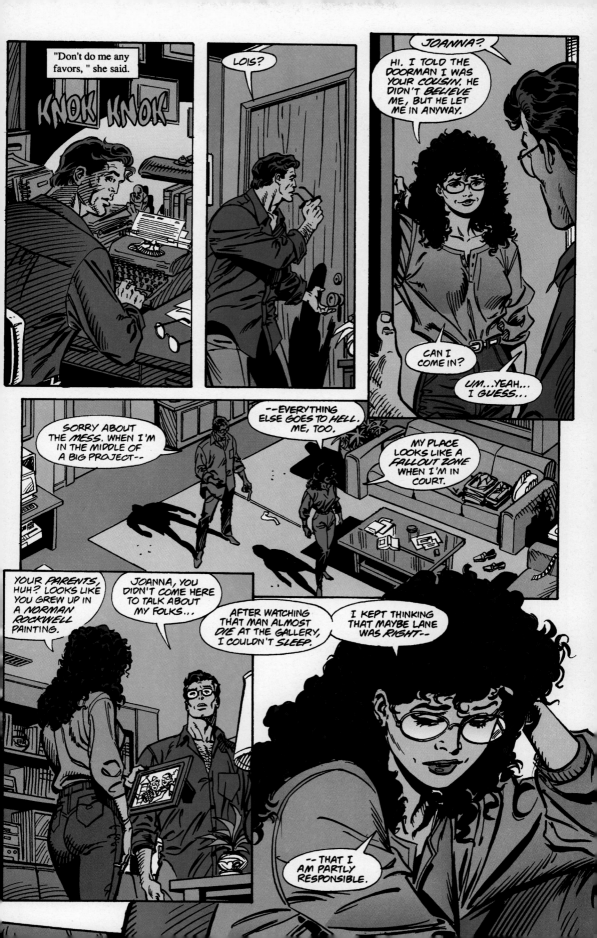

"Don't do me any favors," she said.

KNOK KNOK

LOIS?

JOANNA?

HI. I TOLD THE DOORMAN I WAS YOUR *COUSIN*. HE DIDN'T *BELIEVE* ME, BUT HE LET ME IN ANYWAY.

CAN I COME IN?

UM...YEAH... I GUESS...

SORRY ABOUT THE *MESS*. WHEN I'M IN THE MIDDLE OF A BIG PROJECT--

--EVERYTHING ELSE GOES TO HELL. ME, TOO.

MY PLACE LOOKS LIKE A *FALLOUT ZONE* WHEN I'M IN COURT.

YOUR *PARENTS*, HUH? LOOKS LIKE YOU GREW UP IN A *NORMAN ROCKWELL* PAINTING.

JOANNA, YOU DIDN'T COME HERE TO TALK ABOUT MY FOLKS...

AFTER WATCHING THAT MAN ALMOST *DIE* AT THE GALLERY, I COULDN'T *SLEEP*.

I KEPT THINKING THAT MAYBE LANE WAS *RIGHT*--

-- THAT I AM PARTLY RESPONSIBLE.

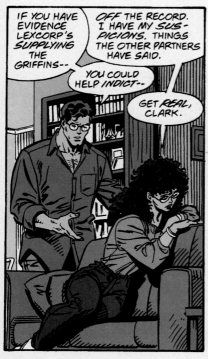

IF YOU HAVE EVIDENCE LEXCORP'S *SUPPLYING* THE *GRIFFINS*--

YOU COULD HELP *INDICT*--

OFF THE RECORD. I HAVE MY *SUSPICIONS.* THINGS THE OTHER PARTNERS HAVE SAID.

GET *REAL,* CLARK.

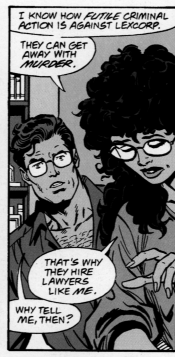

I KNOW HOW *FUTILE* CRIMINAL ACTION IS AGAINST LEXCORP.

THEY CAN GET AWAY WITH *MURDER.*

THAT'S WHY THEY HIRE LAWYERS LIKE *ME.*

WHY TELL ME, THEN?

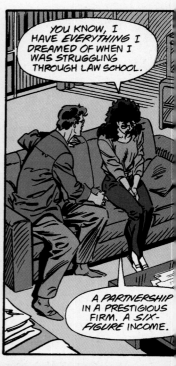

YOU KNOW, I HAVE *EVERYTHING* I DREAMED OF WHEN I WAS STRUGGLING THROUGH LAW SCHOOL.

A *PARTNERSHIP* IN A *PRESTIGIOUS* FIRM. A *SIX-FIGURE* INCOME.

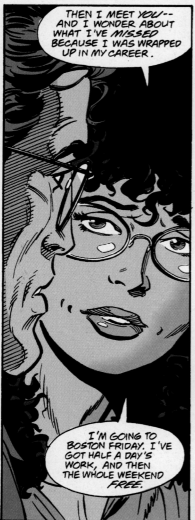

THEN I MEET *YOU*-- AND I WONDER ABOUT WHAT I'VE *MISSED* BECAUSE I WAS WRAPPED UP IN MY CAREER.

I'M GOING TO *BOSTON* FRIDAY. I'VE GOT HALF A DAY'S WORK, AND THEN THE WHOLE WEEKEND *FREE.*

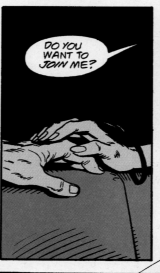

DO YOU WANT TO *JOIN ME?*

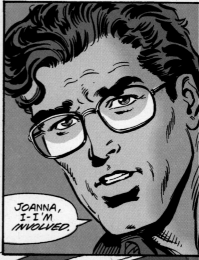

JOANNA, I-I'M *INVOLVED.*

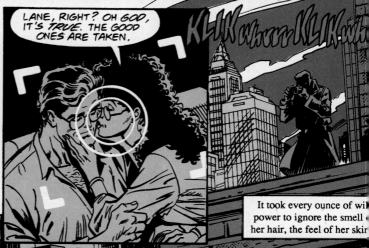

LANE, RIGHT? OH GOD, IT'S *TRUE.* THE GOOD ONES ARE TAKEN.

KLIK *whirr* KLIK *wh*

It took every ounce of wi[ll] power to ignore the smell [of] her hair, the feel of her skin

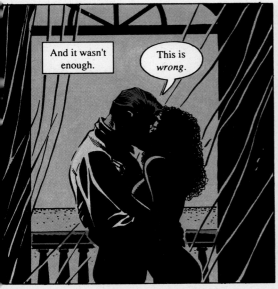

And it wasn't enough.

This is *wrong*.

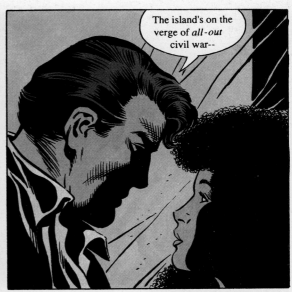

The island's on the verge of *all-out* civil war--

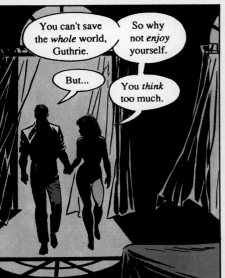

You can't save the *whole* world, Guthrie.

So why not *enjoy* yourself.

But...

You *think* too much.

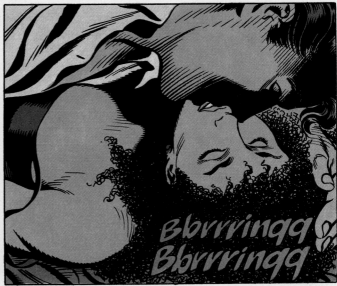

Bbrrringg Bbrrringg

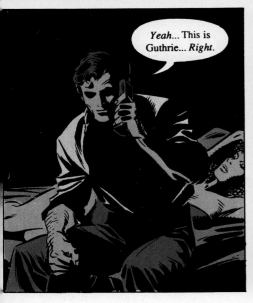

Yeah... This is Guthrie... *Right*.

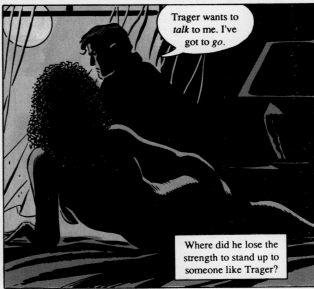

Trager wants to *talk* to me. I've got to *go*.

Where did he lose the strength to stand up to someone like Trager?

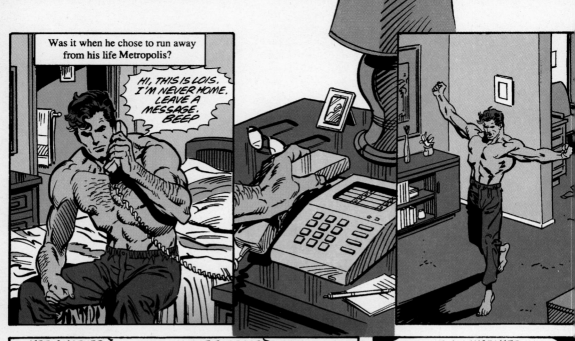

Was it when he chose to run away from his life Metropolis?

HI, THIS IS LOIS. I'M NEVER HOME. LEAVE A MESSAGE. BEEP

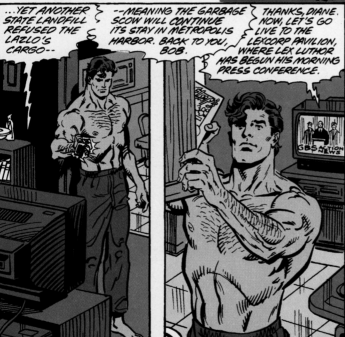

...YET ANOTHER STATE LANDFILL REFUSED THE LAZLO'S CARGO--

--MEANING THE GARBAGE SCOW WILL CONTINUE ITS STAY IN METROPOLIS HARBOR. BACK TO YOU, BOB.

THANKS, DIANE. NOW, LET'S GO LIVE TO THE LEXCORP PAVILION, WHERE LEX LUTHOR HAS BEGUN HIS MORNING PRESS CONFERENCE.

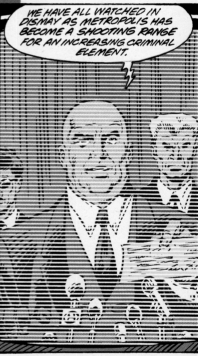

WE HAVE ALL WATCHED IN DISMAY AS METROPOLIS HAS BECOME A SHOOTING RANGE FOR AN INCREASING CRIMINAL ELEMENT.

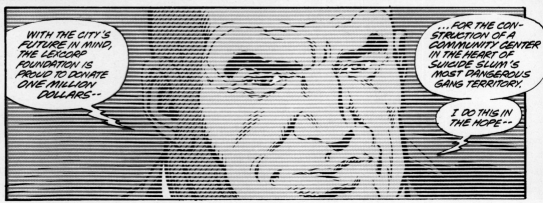

WITH THE CITY'S FUTURE IN MIND, THE LEXCORP FOUNDATION IS PROUD TO DONATE ONE MILLION DOLLARS--

...FOR THE CONSTRUCTION OF A COMMUNITY CENTER IN THE HEART OF SUICIDE SLUM'S MOST DANGEROUS GANG TERRITORY.

I DO THIS IN THE HOPE--

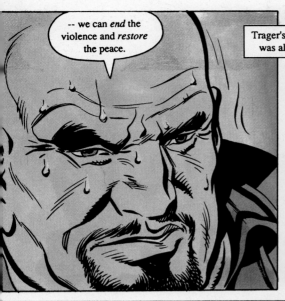

-- we can *end* the violence and *restore* the peace.

Trager's practiced sincerity was almost convincing.

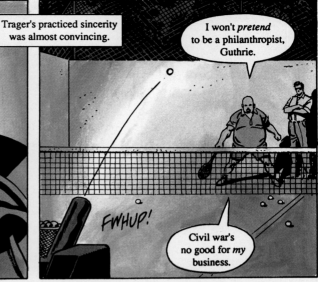

I won't *pretend* to be a philanthropist, Guthrie.

FWHUP!

Civil war's no good for *my* business.

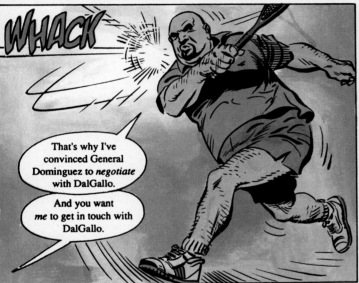

WHACK

That's why I've convinced General Dominguez to *negotiate* with DalGallo.

And you want *me* to get in touch with DalGallo.

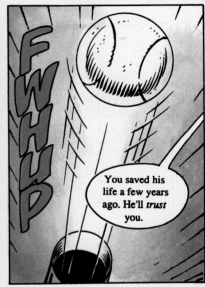

FWHUP

You saved his life a few years ago. He'll *trust* you.

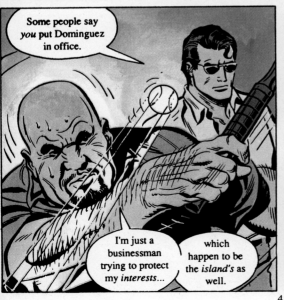

Some people say *you* put Dominguez in office.

I'm just a businessman trying to protect my *interests*...

which happen to be the *island's* as well.

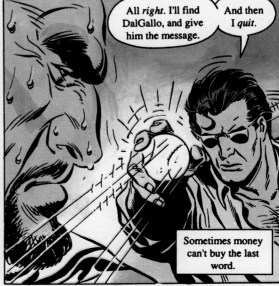

All *right*. I'll find DalGallo, and give him the message.

And then I *quit*.

Sometimes money can't buy the last word.

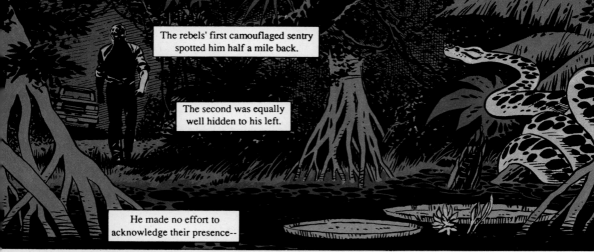

The rebels' first camouflaged sentry spotted him half a mile back.

The second was equally well hidden to his left.

He made no effort to acknowledge their presence--

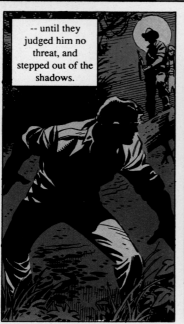

-- until they judged him no threat, and stepped out of the shadows.

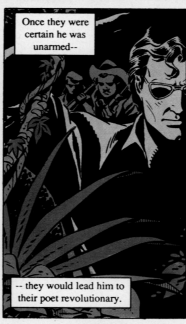

Once they were certain he was unarmed--

-- they would lead him to their poet revolutionary.

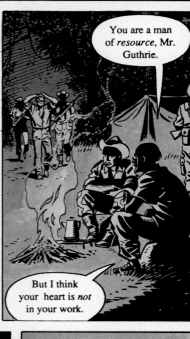

You are a man of *resource*, Mr. Guthrie.

But I think your heart is *not* in your work.

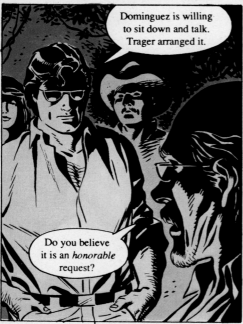

Dominguez is willing to sit down and talk. Trager arranged it.

Do you believe it is an *honorable* request?

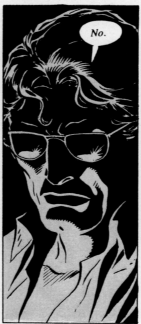

No.

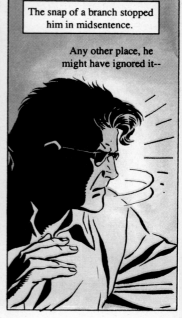

The snap of a branch stopped him in midsentence.

Any other place, he might have ignored it--

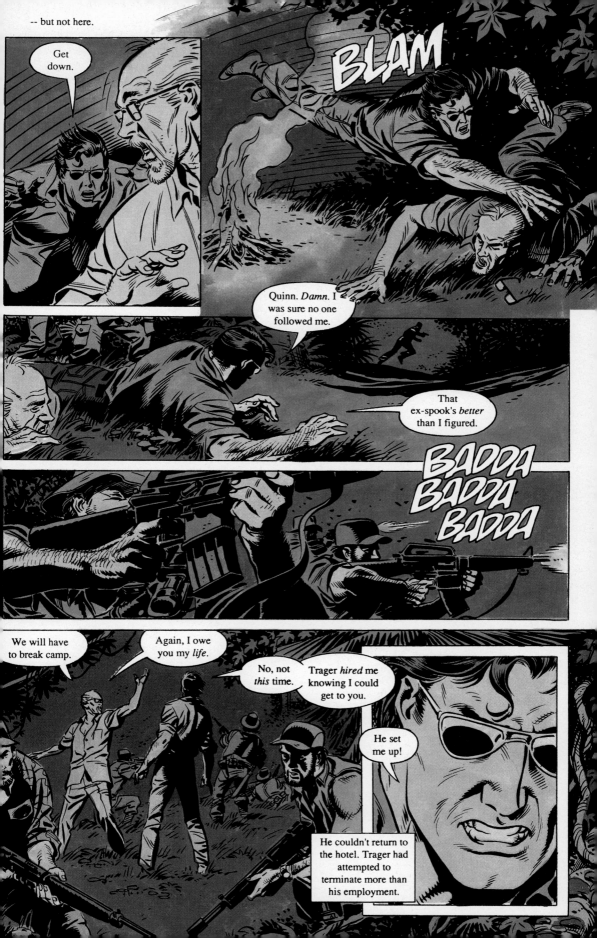

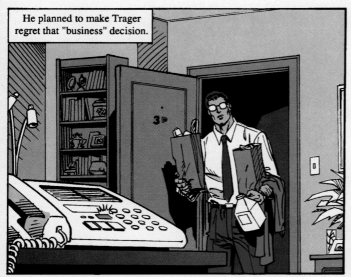

He planned to make Trager regret that "business" decision.

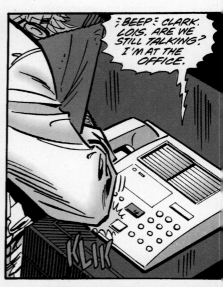

≒BEEP≒ CLARK. LOIS, ARE WE STILL TALKING? I'M AT THE OFFICE.

KLIK

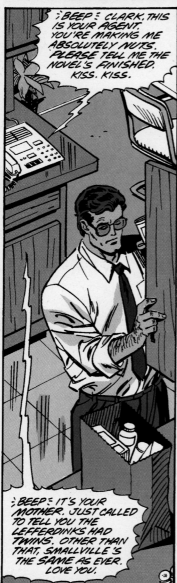

≒BEEP≒ CLARK, THIS IS YOUR AGENT. YOU'RE MAKING ME ABSOLUTELY NUTS. PLEASE TELL ME THE NOVEL'S FINISHED. KISS. KISS.

≒BEEP≒ IT'S YOUR MOTHER. JUST CALLED TO TELL YOU THE LEFFERDINKS HAD TWINS. OTHER THAN THAT, SMALLVILLE'S THE SAME AS EVER. LOVE YOU.

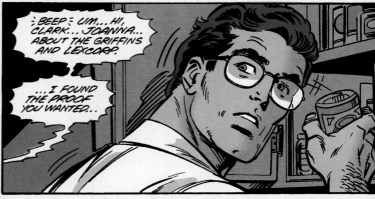

≒BEEP≒ UM... HI, CLARK... JOANNA... ABOUT THE GRIFFINS AND LEXCORP.

...I FOUND THE PROOF YOU WANTED...

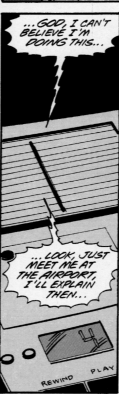

...GOD, I CAN'T BELIEVE I'M DOING THIS...

...LOOK, JUST MEET ME AT THE AIRPORT, I'LL EXPLAIN THEN...

REWIND   PLAY

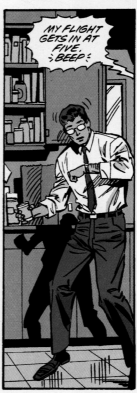

MY FLIGHT GETS IN AT FIVE. ≒BEEP≒

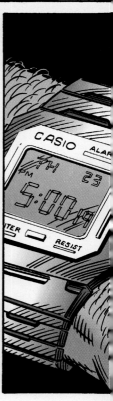

CASIO   ALAR

5:00

44

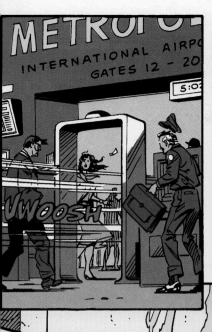

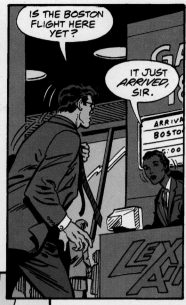

IS THE BOSTON FLIGHT HERE YET?

IT JUST ARRIVED, SIR.

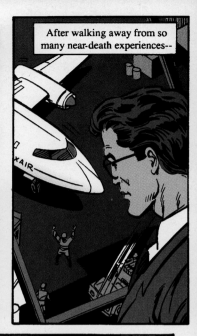

After walking away from so many near-death experiences--

-- he had convinced himself he was *invulnerable*--

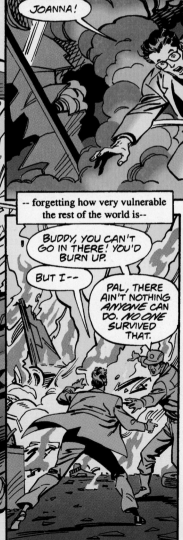

JOANNA!

-- forgetting how very vulnerable the rest of the world is--

BUDDY, YOU CAN'T GO IN THERE! YOU'D BURN UP.

BUT I--

PAL, THERE AIN'T NOTHING ANYONE CAN DO. *NO ONE* SURVIVED THAT.

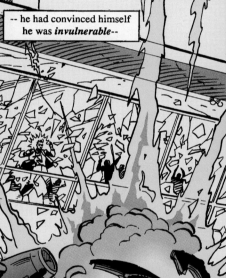

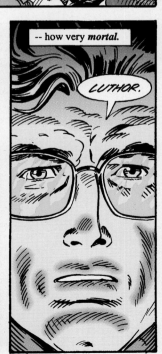

-- how very *mortal*.

LUTHOR.

45

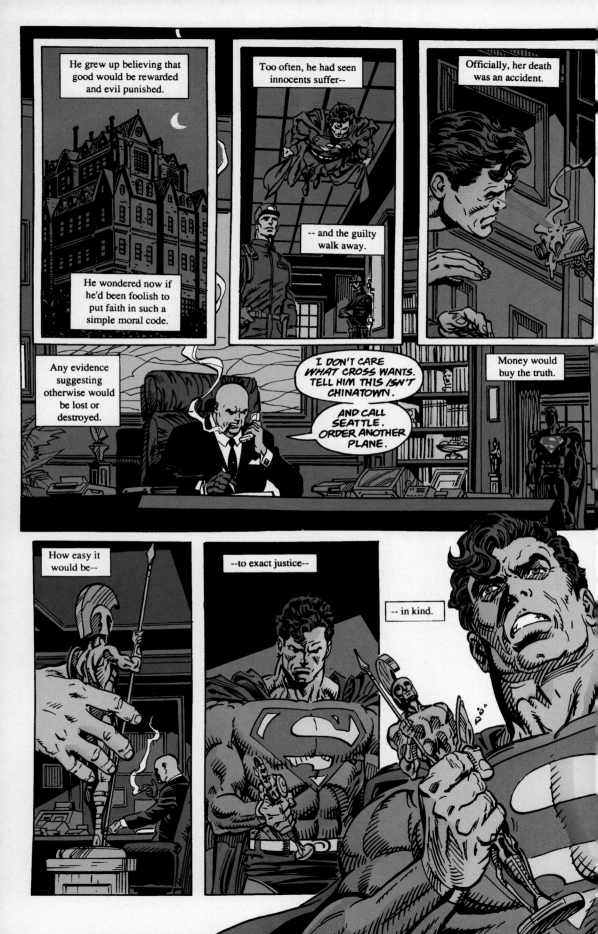

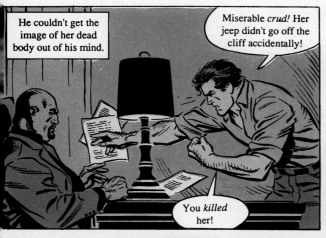

He couldn't get the image of her dead body out of his mind.

Miserable *crud!* Her jeep didn't go off the cliff accidentally!

You *killed* her!

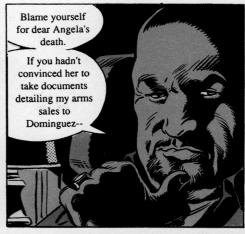

Blame yourself for dear Angela's death.

If you hadn't convinced her to take documents detailing my arms sales to Dominguez--

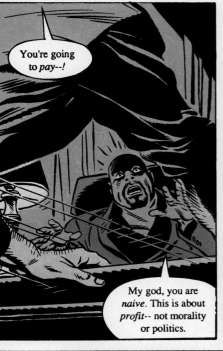

You're going to *pay--!*

My god, you are *naive*. This is about *profit*-- not morality or politics.

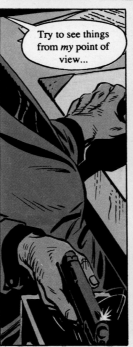

Try to see things from *my* point of view...

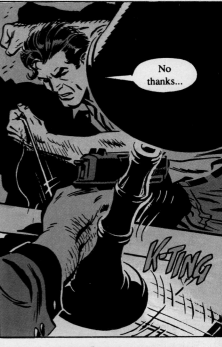

No thanks...

K-TING

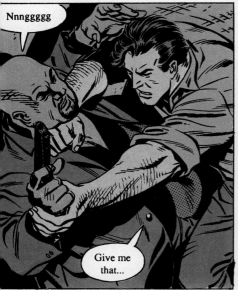

Nnnggggg

Give me that...

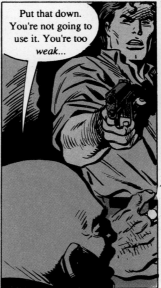

Put that down. You're not going to use it. You're too *weak*...

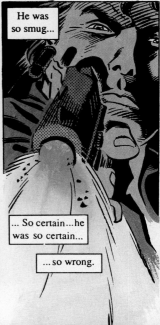

He was so smug...

... So certain...he was so certain...

... so wrong.

47

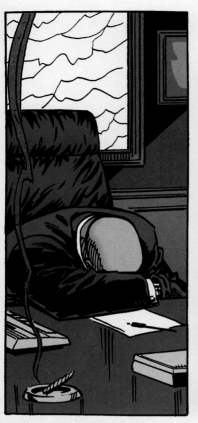
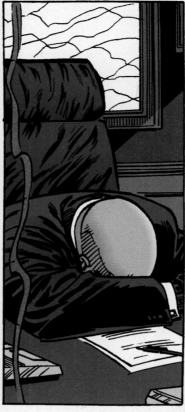
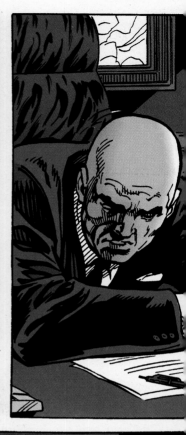
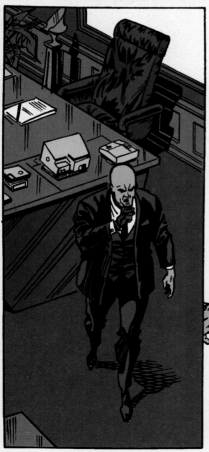
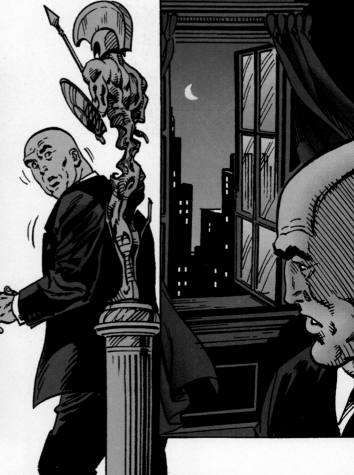

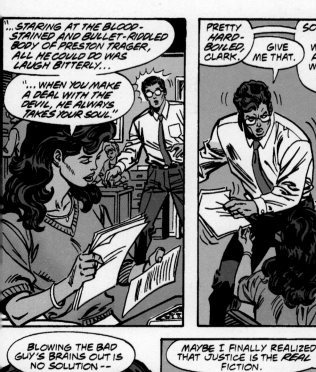

"...STARING AT THE BLOOD-STAINED AND BULLET-RIDDLED BODY OF PRESTON TRAGER, ALL HE COULD DO WAS LAUGH BITTERLY...

"...WHEN YOU MAKE A DEAL WITH THE DEVIL, HE ALWAYS TAKES YOUR SOUL."

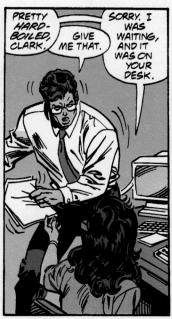

PRETTY HARD-BOILED, CLARK.

GIVE ME THAT.

SORRY. I WAS WAITING, AND IT WAS ON YOUR DESK.

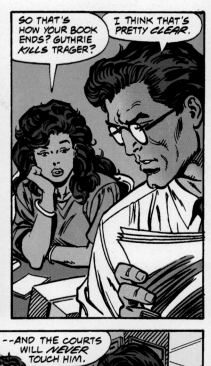

SO THAT'S HOW YOUR BOOK ENDS? GUTHRIE KILLS TRAGER?

I THINK THAT'S PRETTY CLEAR.

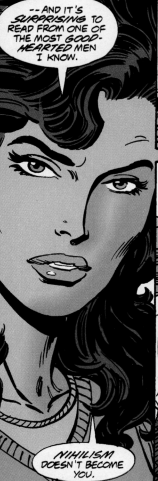

BLOWING THE BAD GUY'S BRAINS OUT IS NO SOLUTION --

-- AND IT'S SURPRISING TO READ FROM ONE OF THE MOST GOOD-HEARTED MEN I KNOW.

NIHILISM DOESN'T BECOME YOU.

MAYBE I FINALLY REALIZED THAT JUSTICE IS THE REAL FICTION.

LUTHOR SUPPLIES WEAPONS TO STREET GANGS, TURNS METROPOLIS INTO A WAR ZONE--

--AND THE COURTS WILL NEVER TOUCH HIM.

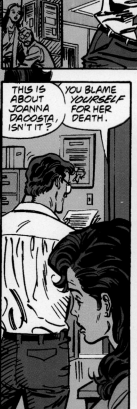

THIS IS ABOUT JOANNA DACOSTA, ISN'T IT?

YOU BLAME YOURSELF FOR HER DEATH.

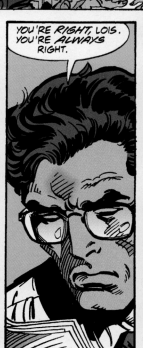

YOU'RE RIGHT, LOIS. YOU'RE ALWAYS RIGHT.

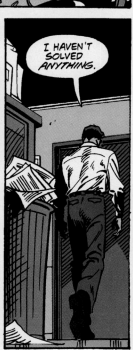

I HAVEN'T SOLVED ANYTHING.

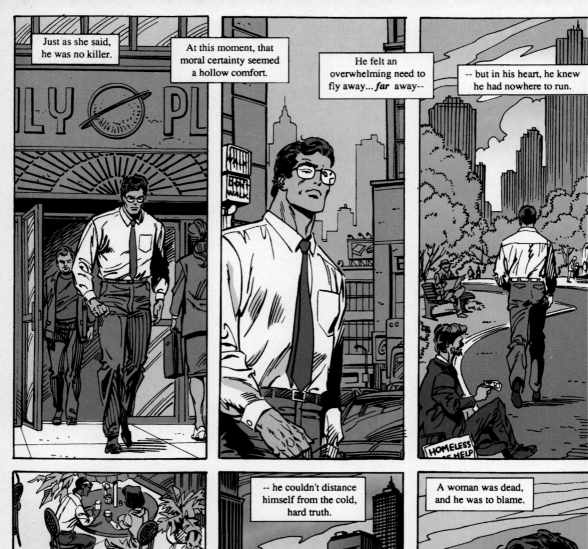

Just as she said, he was no killer.

At this moment, that moral certainty seemed a hollow comfort.

He felt an overwhelming need to fly away... *far* away--

-- but in his heart, he knew he had nowhere to run.

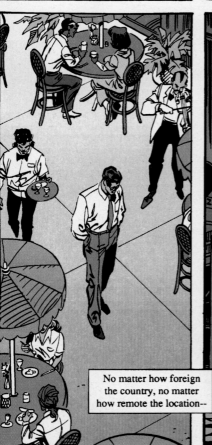

No matter how foreign the country, no matter how remote the location--

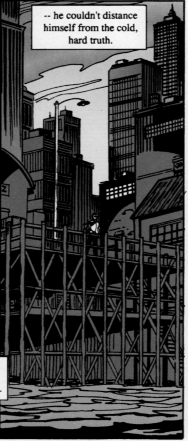

-- he couldn't distance himself from the cold, hard truth.

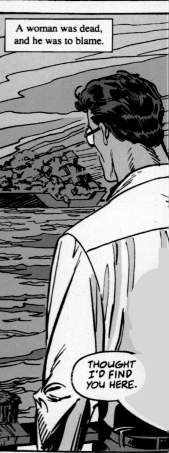

A woman was dead, and he was to blame.

THOUGHT I'D FIND YOU HERE.

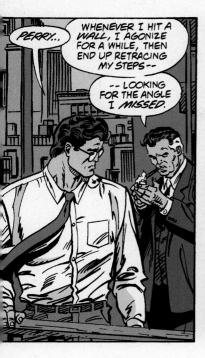

PERRY...

WHENEVER I HIT A WALL, I AGONIZE FOR A WHILE, THEN END UP RETRACING MY STEPS--

--LOOKING FOR THE ANGLE I MISSED.

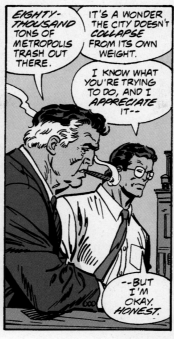

EIGHTY-THOUSAND TONS OF METROPOLIS TRASH OUT THERE.

IT'S A WONDER THE CITY DOESN'T COLLAPSE FROM ITS OWN WEIGHT.

I KNOW WHAT YOU'RE TRYING TO DO, AND I APPRECIATE IT--

--BUT I'M OKAY. HONEST.

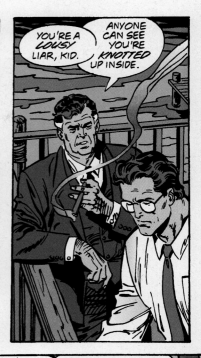

YOU'RE A LOUSY LIAR, KID.

ANYONE CAN SEE YOU'RE KNOTTED UP INSIDE.

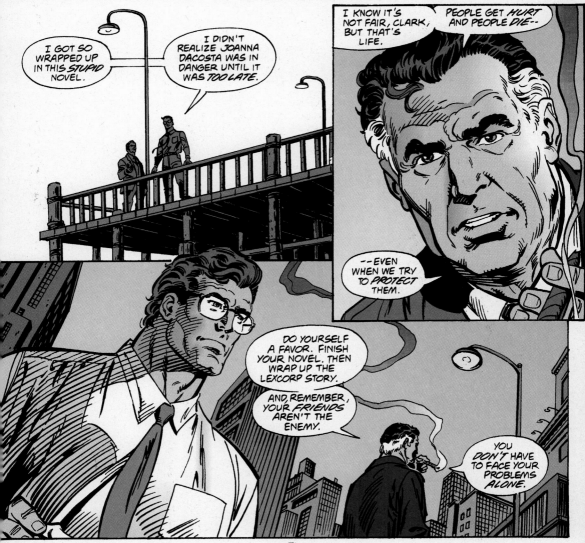

I GOT SO WRAPPED UP IN THIS STUPID NOVEL.

I DIDN'T REALIZE JOANNA DACOSTA WAS IN DANGER UNTIL IT WAS TOO LATE.

I KNOW IT'S NOT FAIR, CLARK, BUT THAT'S LIFE.

PEOPLE GET HURT AND PEOPLE DIE--

--EVEN WHEN WE TRY TO PROTECT THEM.

DO YOURSELF A FAVOR. FINISH YOUR NOVEL, THEN WRAP UP THE LEXCORP STORY.

AND, REMEMBER, YOUR FRIENDS AREN'T THE ENEMY.

YOU DON'T HAVE TO FACE YOUR PROBLEMS ALONE.

Hawkins didn't need to be asked twice.

If Guthrie intended to knock Trager out of his ivory tower, the old sailor was prepared to help him, come hell or high water—

—and with Hurricane Simone headed directly for Corto Maltese, the latter seemed more than likely.

Shoulda *killed* that bald vulture when you had the chance.

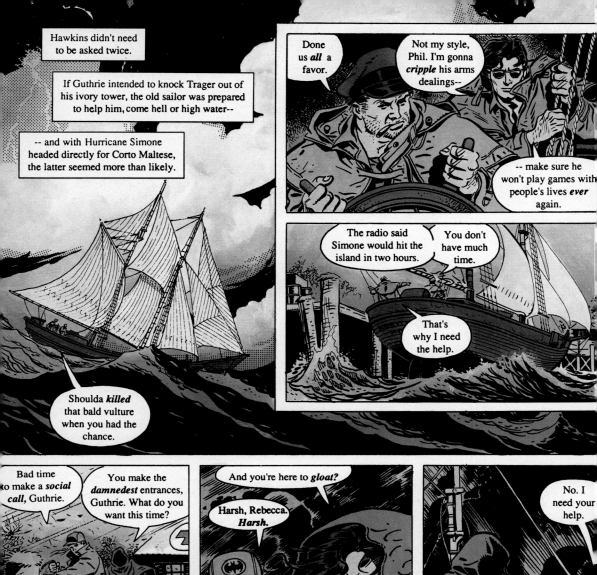

Done us *all* a favor.

Not my style, Phil. I'm gonna *cripple* his arms dealings—

—make sure he won't play games with people's lives *ever* again.

The radio said Simone would hit the island in two hours.

You don't have much time.

That's why I need the help.

Bad time to make a *social call*, Guthrie.

You make the *damnedest* entrances, Guthrie. What do you want this time?

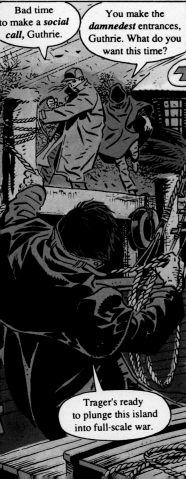

Trager's ready to plunge this island into full-scale war.

And you're here to *gloat?*

Harsh, Rebecca. *Harsh.*

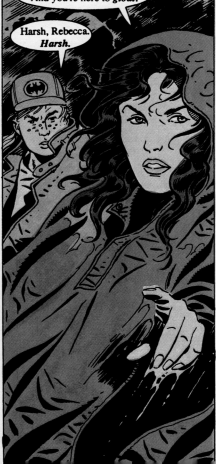

No. I need your help.

My help?

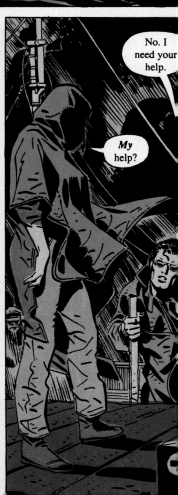

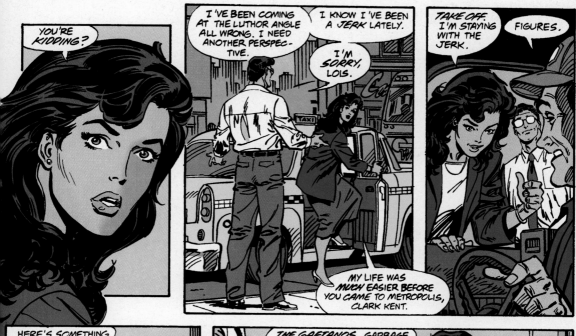

YOU'RE KIDDING?

I'VE BEEN COMING AT THE LUTHOR ANGLE ALL WRONG. I NEED ANOTHER PERSPECTIVE.

I KNOW I'VE BEEN A JERK LATELY.

I'M SORRY, LOIS.

TAKE OFF. I'M STAYING WITH THE JERK.

FIGURES.

MY LIFE WAS MUCH EASIER BEFORE YOU CAME TO METROPOLIS, CLARK KENT.

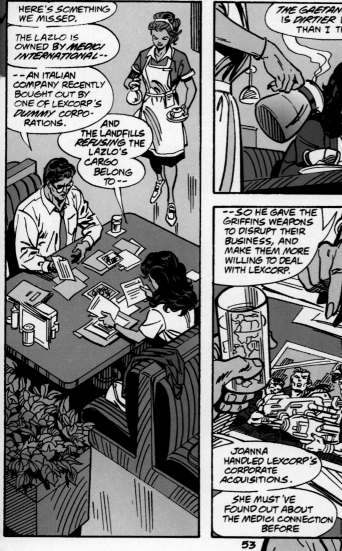

HERE'S SOMETHING WE MISSED.

THE LAZLO IS OWNED BY MEDICI INTERNATIONAL--

--AN ITALIAN COMPANY RECENTLY BOUGHT OUT BY ONE OF LEXCORP'S DUMMY CORPORATIONS.

AND THE LANDFILLS REFUSING THE LAZLO'S CARGO BELONG TO--

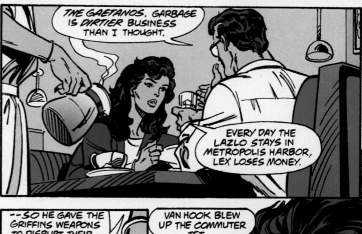

THE GAETANOS. GARBAGE IS DIRTIER BUSINESS THAN I THOUGHT.

EVERY DAY THE LAZLO STAYS IN METROPOLIS HARBOR, LEX LOSES MONEY.

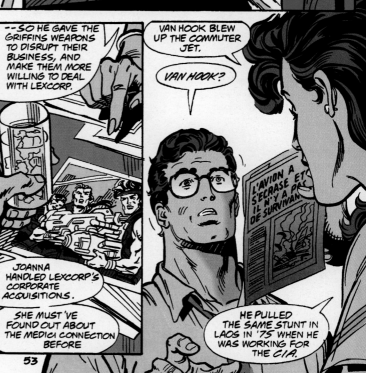

--SO HE GAVE THE GRIFFINS WEAPONS TO DISRUPT THEIR BUSINESS, AND MAKE THEM MORE WILLING TO DEAL WITH LEXCORP.

JOANNA HANDLED LEXCORP'S CORPORATE ACQUISITIONS.

SHE MUST'VE FOUND OUT ABOUT THE MEDICI CONNECTION BEFORE

VAN HOOK BLEW UP THE COMMUTER JET.

VAN HOOK?

L'AVION A S'ECRASE ET IL N'Y A PA DE SURVIVAN

HE PULLED THE SAME STUNT IN LAOS IN '75 WHEN HE WAS WORKING FOR THE CIA.

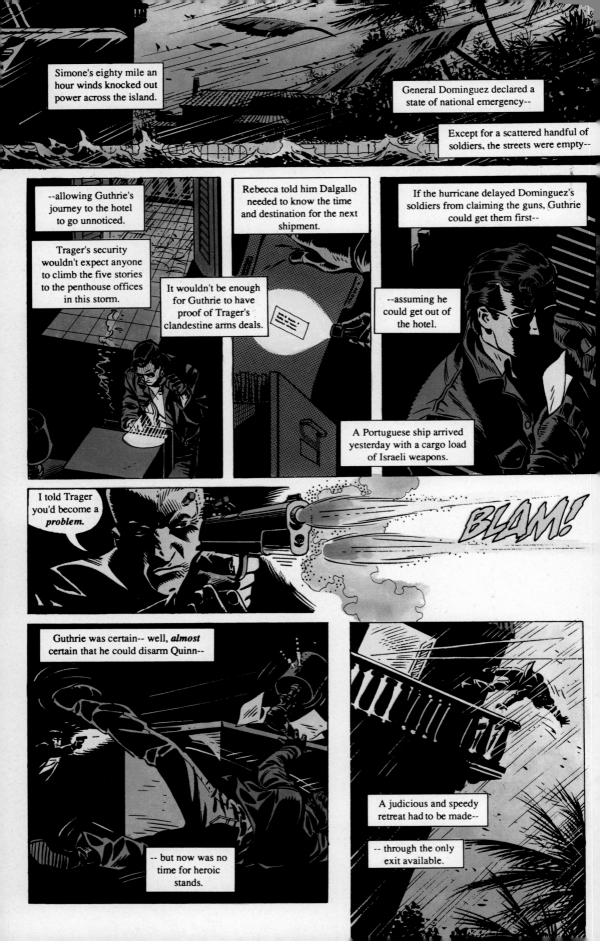

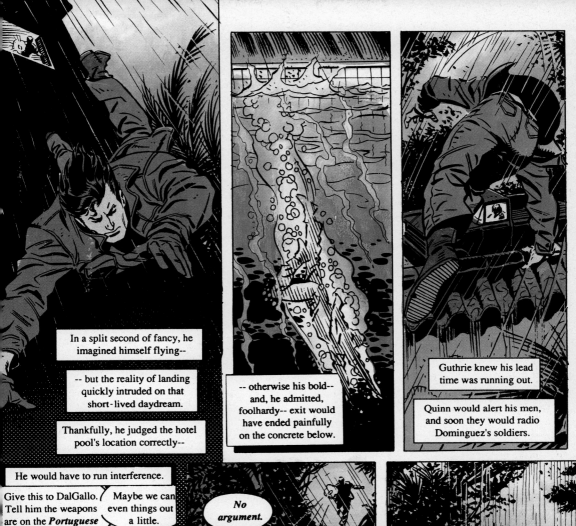

In a split second of fancy, he imagined himself flying--

-- but the reality of landing quickly intruded on that short-lived daydream.

Thankfully, he judged the hotel pool's location correctly--

-- otherwise his bold-- and, he admitted, foolhardy-- exit would have ended painfully on the concrete below.

Guthrie knew his lead time was running out.

Quinn would alert his men, and soon they would radio Dominguez's soldiers.

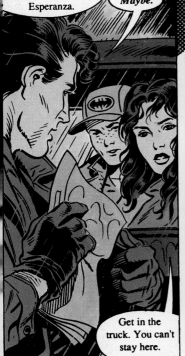

He would have to run interference.

Give this to DalGallo. Tell him the weapons are on the *Portuguese* freighter docked at Esperanza.

Maybe we can even things out a little.

Maybe.

Get in the truck. You can't stay here.

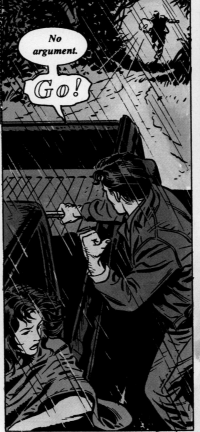

No argument.

Go!

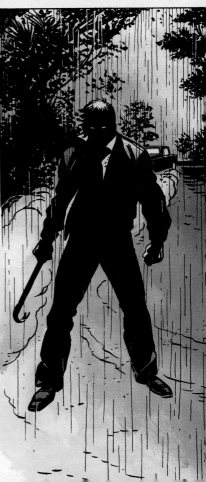

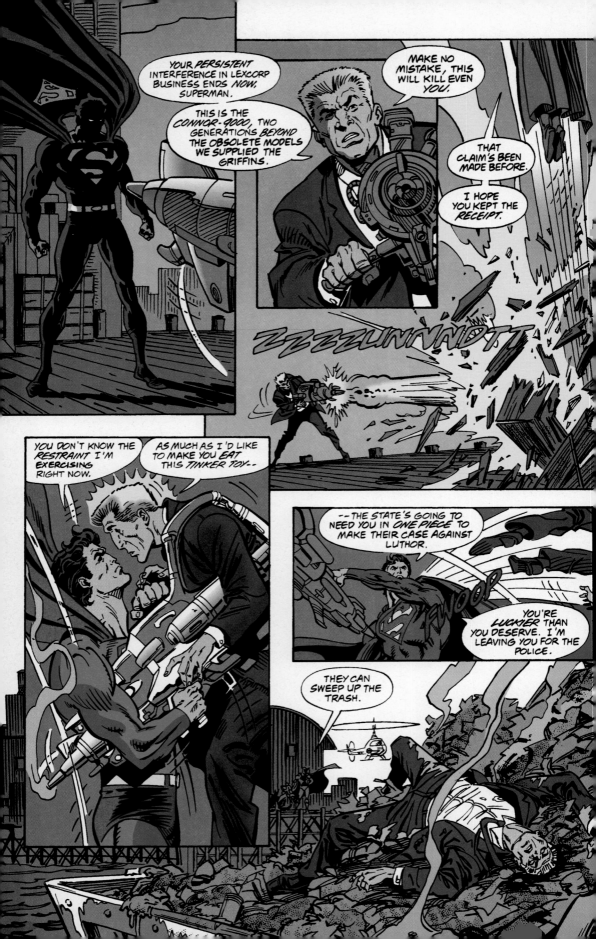

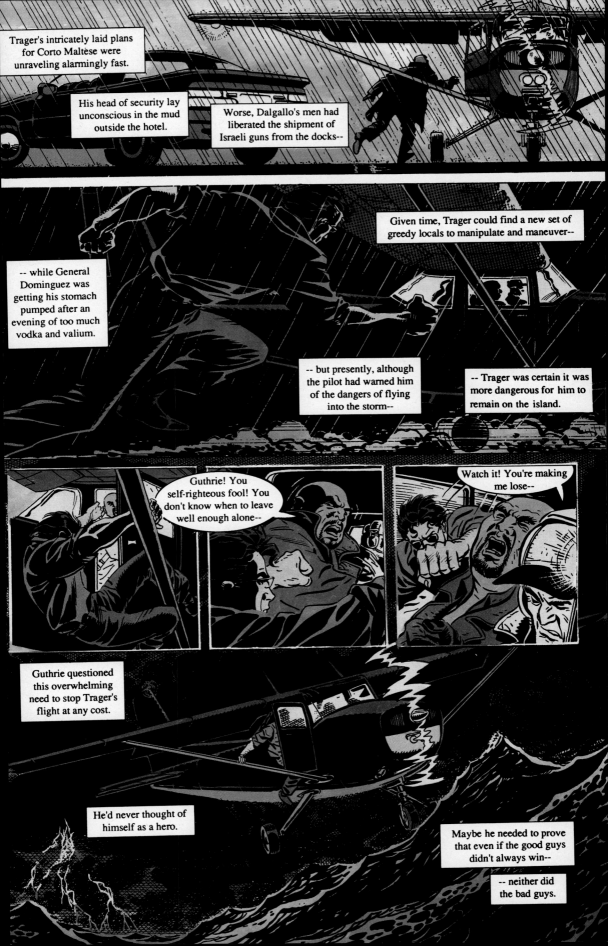

Trager's intricately laid plans for Corto Maltèse were unraveling alarmingly fast.

His head of security lay unconscious in the mud outside the hotel.

Worse, Dalgallo's men had liberated the shipment of Israeli guns from the docks--

Given time, Trager could find a new set of greedy locals to manipulate and maneuver--

-- while General Dominguez was getting his stomach pumped after an evening of too much vodka and valium.

-- but presently, although the pilot had warned him of the dangers of flying into the storm--

-- Trager was certain it was more dangerous for him to remain on the island.

Guthrie! You self-righteous fool! You don't know when to leave well enough alone--

Watch it! You're making me lose--

Guthrie questioned this overwhelming need to stop Trager's flight at any cost.

He'd never thought of himself as a hero.

Maybe he needed to prove that even if the good guys didn't always win--

-- neither did the bad guys.

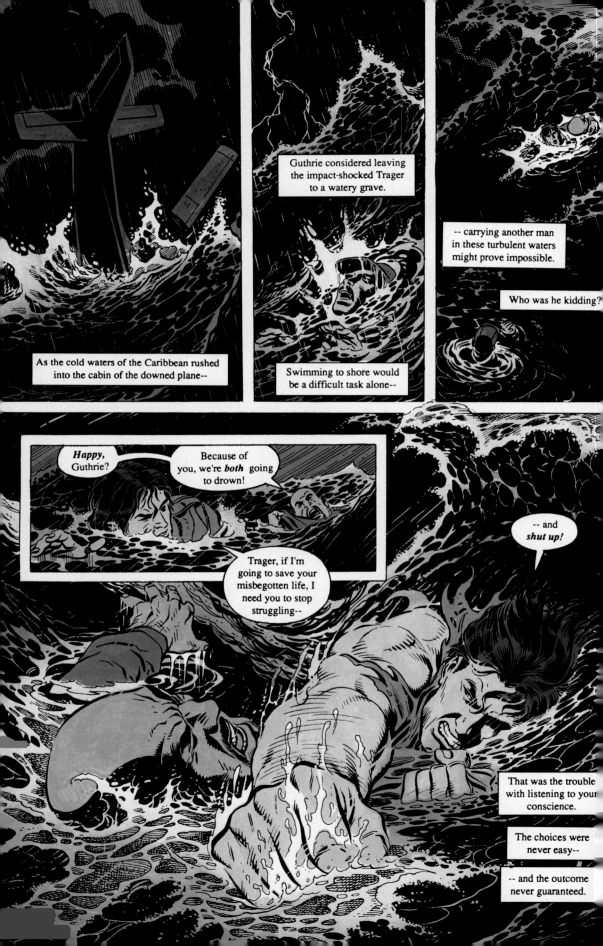

Guthrie considered leaving the impact-shocked Trager to a watery grave.

-- carrying another man in these turbulent waters might prove impossible.

Who was he kidding?

As the cold waters of the Caribbean rushed into the cabin of the downed plane--

Swimming to shore would be a difficult task alone--

Happy, Guthrie?

Because of you, we're *both* going to drown!

Trager, if I'm going to save your misbegotten life, I need you to stop struggling--

-- and *shut up!*

That was the trouble with listening to your conscience.

The choices were never easy--

-- and the outcome never guaranteed.

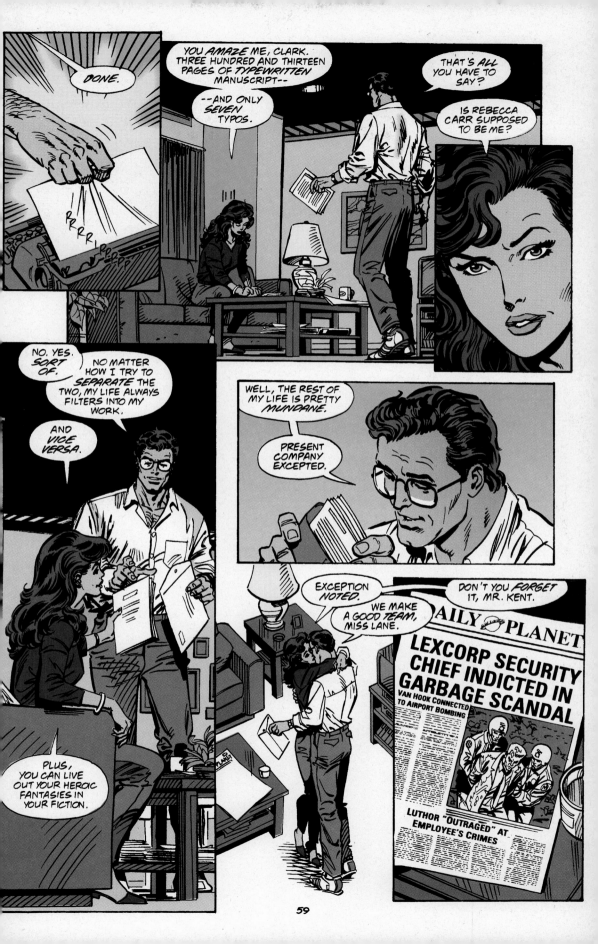

DONE.

YOU *AMAZE* ME, CLARK. THREE HUNDRED AND THIRTEEN PAGES OF *TYPEWRITTEN* MANUSCRIPT--

--AND ONLY *SEVEN* TYPOS.

THAT'S *ALL* YOU HAVE TO *SAY?*

IS REBECCA CARR SUPPOSED TO BE ME?

NO. YES. *SORT OF.*

NO MATTER HOW I TRY TO *SEPARATE* THE TWO, MY LIFE ALWAYS FILTERS INTO MY WORK.

AND *VICE VERSA.*

WELL, THE REST OF MY LIFE IS PRETTY *MUNDANE.*

PRESENT COMPANY *EXCEPTED.*

PLUS, YOU CAN LIVE OUT YOUR *HEROIC* FANTASIES IN YOUR FICTION.

EXCEPTION *NOTED.*

WE MAKE A GOOD *TEAM,* MISS LANE.

DON'T YOU *FORGET* IT, MR. KENT.

DAILY PLANET

LEXCORP SECURITY CHIEF INDICTED IN GARBAGE SCANDAL

VAN HOOK CONNECTED TO AIRPORT BOMBING

LUTHOR "OUTRAGED" AT EMPLOYEE'S CRIMES

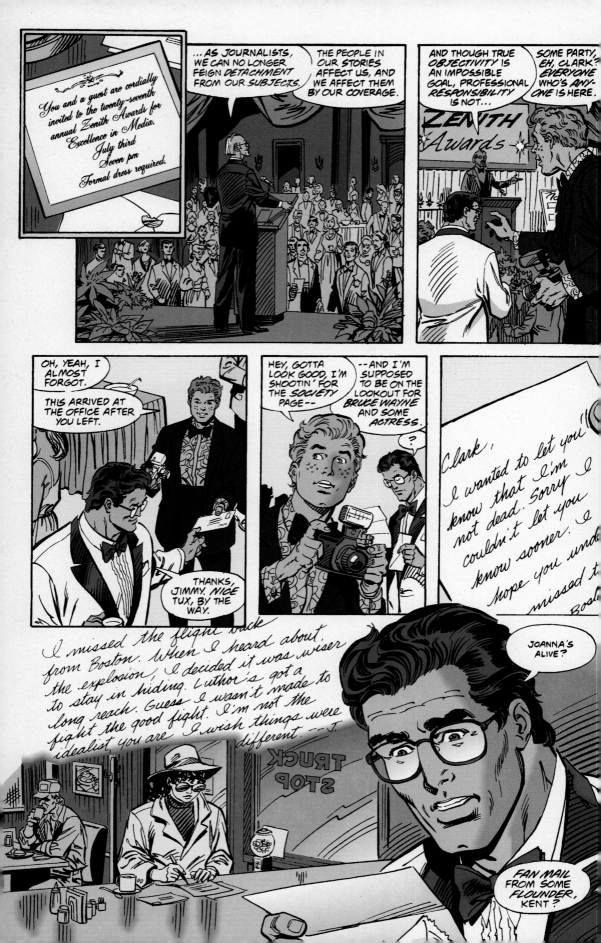

You and a guest are cordially invited to the twenty-seventh annual Zenith Awards for Excellence in Media.
July third
Seven pm
Formal dress required.

...AS JOURNALISTS, WE CAN NO LONGER FEIGN *DETACHMENT* FROM OUR *SUBJECTS.*

THE PEOPLE IN OUR STORIES AFFECT US, AND WE AFFECT THEM BY OUR COVERAGE.

AND THOUGH TRUE *OBJECTIVITY* IS AN IMPOSSIBLE GOAL, PROFESSIONAL *RESPONSIBILITY* IS NOT...

SOME PARTY, EH, CLARK? *EVERYONE* WHO'S *ANY-ONE* IS HERE.

ZENITH Awards

OH, YEAH, I ALMOST FORGOT.

THIS ARRIVED AT THE OFFICE AFTER YOU LEFT.

THANKS, JIMMY. *NICE* TUX, BY THE WAY.

HEY, GOTTA LOOK GOOD, I'M SHOOTIN' FOR THE *SOCIETY* PAGE--

--AND I'M SUPPOSED TO BE ON THE LOOKOUT FOR *BRUCE WAYNE* AND SOME ACTRESS.

?

Clark,
I wanted to let you know that I'm not dead. Sorry I couldn't let you know sooner. I hope you und--
missed t
Bost

I missed the flight back from Boston. When I heard about the explosion, I decided it was wiser to stay in hiding. Luthor's got a long reach. Guess I wasn't made to fight the good fight. I'm not the idealist you are. I wish things were different. --J.

TRUCK STOP

JOANNA'S ALIVE?

FAN MAIL FROM SOME *FLOUNDER,* KENT?

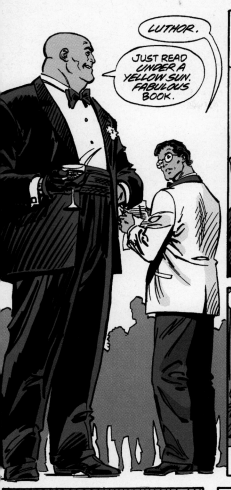

LUTHOR.

JUST READ *UNDER A YELLOW SUN.* FABULOUS BOOK.

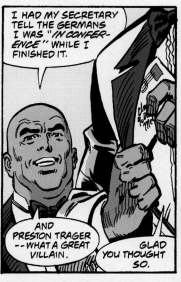

I HAD MY SECRETARY TELL THE GERMANS I WAS *"IN CONFERENCE"* WHILE I FINISHED IT.

AND PRESTON TRAGER -- WHAT A GREAT VILLAIN.

GLAD YOU THOUGHT SO.

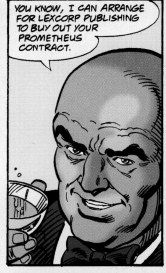

YOU KNOW, I CAN ARRANGE FOR LEXCORP PUBLISHING TO BUY OUT YOUR PROMETHEUS CONTRACT.

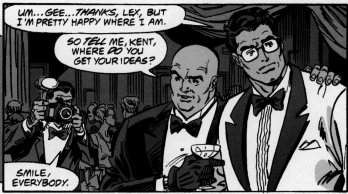

UM...GEE...*THANKS,* LEX, BUT I'M PRETTY HAPPY WHERE I AM.

SO *TELL* ME, KENT, WHERE *DO* YOU GET YOUR IDEAS?

SMILE, EVERYBODY.

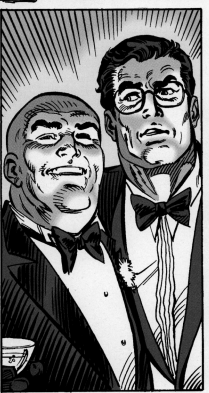

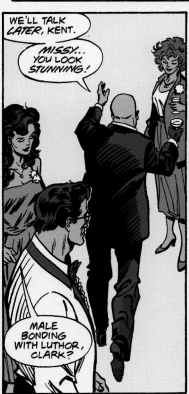

WE'LL TALK *LATER,* KENT.

MISSY... YOU LOOK STUNNING!

MALE BONDING WITH LUTHOR, CLARK?

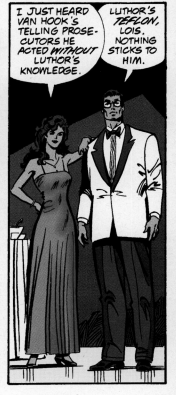

I JUST HEARD VAN HOOK'S TELLING PROSECUTORS HE ACTED *WITHOUT* LUTHOR'S KNOWLEDGE.

LUTHOR'S *TEFLON,* LOIS. NOTHING STICKS TO HIM.

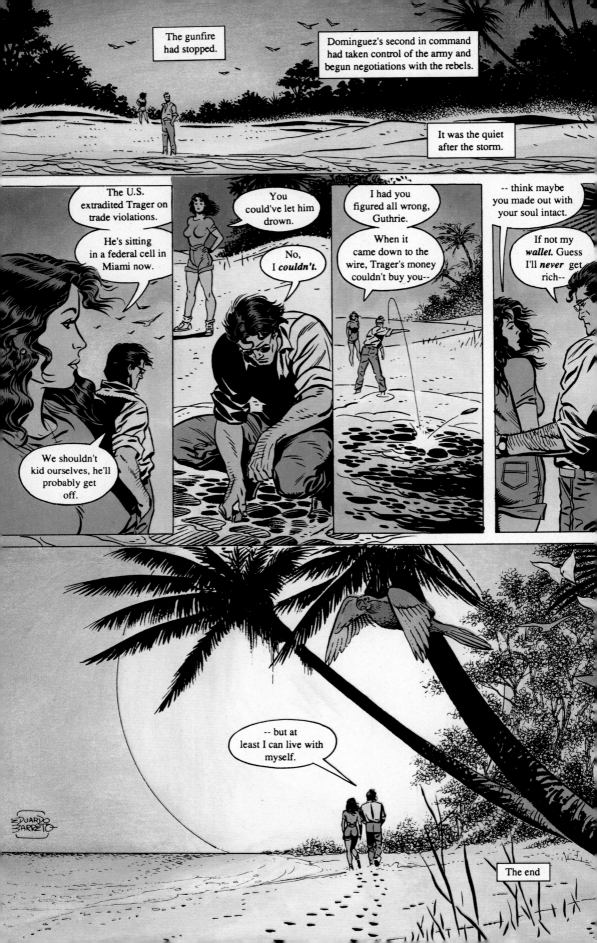

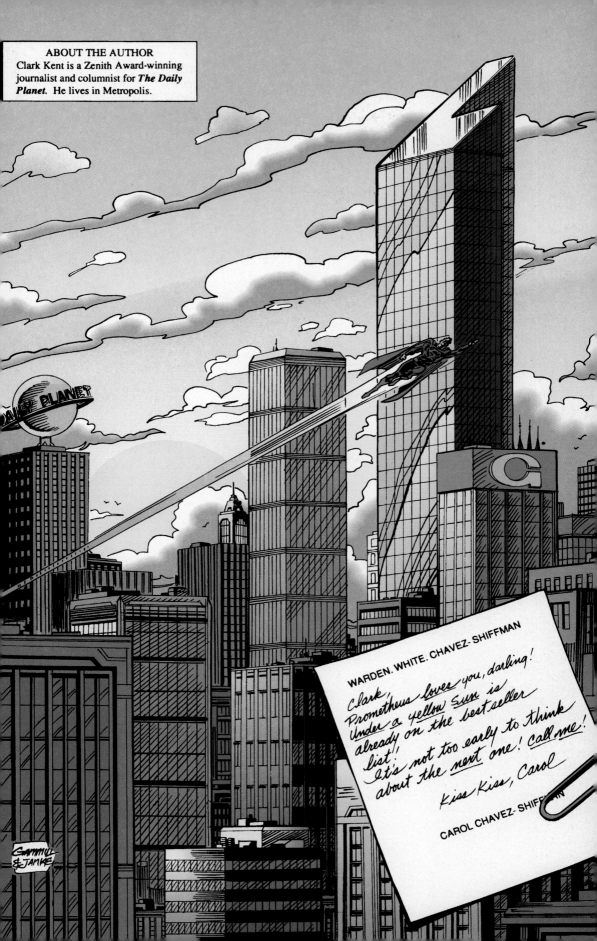

*The author would like to thank the following people,
without whom* UNDER A YELLOW SUN
would never have come to be:

JOHN FRANCIS MOORE
Writer

EDUARDO BARRETO
Artist
NOVEL SEQUENCE

KERRY GAMMILL
Penciller
METROPOLIS SEQUENCE

DENNIS JANKE
Inker
METROPOLIS SEQUENCE

SHERILYN VAN VALKENBURGH
Full Process Color
NOVEL SEQUENCE

GLENN WHITMORE
Color Guides
METROPOLIS SEQUENCE

Superman created by
JERRY SIEGEL & JOE SHUSTER